UNDERSTANDING REVELATION

UNDERSTANDING REVELATION

*A preacher looks at the
End-time message of the
last book of the Bible*

Paul Langham

Terra Nova Publications

First published in Great Britain in 2005
by

Terra Nova Publications International Ltd
PO Box 2400, Bradford on Avon, Wiltshire BA15 2YN

Registered Office (not for trade):
21 St Thomas Street, Bristol BS1 6JS

Cover design by LionHudson
Cover photograph by Alan Bedding

ISBN 1 90194 935 4

Printed in Great Britain
by Bookmarque Ltd, Croydon

Contents

In memory of my father
John Godfrey Langham (1922 – 2002)
who first showed me what it is
to understand Christian truth
and who remained throughout his life
a model of Christ likeness

Preface

'The world at its worst needs a church at its best.' I am not sure where I first heard or read these words, but they have stayed with me. Each reader of this book will have his or her own reasons for picking it up. But I hope that one of the reasons might be because the Book of Revelation describes the world at its worst, and aims to help us be the church at its best. I pray that this book may be an aid in that process.

Understanding Revelation is based on a series of sermons I preached in the autumn of 1999, as our world geared itself for the celebration of a new millennium. In converting that series into a book, I have tried to maintain something of the flavour of the preached material, and have retained the prayers used then at the end of most of the chapters. I was drawn to preach on the End times and the Christian hope of eternity largely because the Christian community today seems either completely to ignore it or to feed upon 'popular' but sub-biblical and sensationalist interpretations of Revelation. These are the books that claim to identify the beast as a specific individual or institution, or to map out a detailed time chart for the end of earth history. Given that Jesus himself, in the days before he died, when asked by his followers, 'What will be the sign of your coming and of the end of the age?' responded immediately with the warning, 'Watch out that no one deceives you', and then went on to warn that the End times would include major apostasy within the church, we must beware the danger of false thinking on this subject. (See Matthew 24:3f and vv. 10–12).

For example, how many members of our churches today are aware that heaven is not the eternal home of the Christian believer? How many Christians today are rather, in the words of St Peter, 'looking forward to a new heaven and a new earth, the home of righteousness?' (2 Peter 3:13). Influenced by centuries of 'theology' based more on Greek thought than biblical truth, even Christians today commonly imagine the afterlife as a floating, insubstantial existence characterised by cloud, wings and harps. But I am excited by the biblical hope of a gloriously renewed physical creation and cosmos, where, through the saving death and resurrection of Jesus Christ, I will live in harmony with myself, my fellow redeemed human beings and my Creator —and have a brand new body into the bargain! Heaven as it currently exists is in fact a waiting room for those believers who die before the return of Christ.

Or consider the modern concept of the rapture current in books such as the 'Left Behind' series of novels, in which Jesus firstly returns suddenly and secretly to whisk believers away from earth before the predicted tribulation upon earth, before returning later in visible triumph. The concept is completely unbiblical —the very fact that it was unknown before about 1830 should give us pause for thought! Yet millions of Christians around the world are now convinced that, whatever times of trouble are visited upon the earth in its final days, those Christians alive at the time will be whisked away in a 'secret' rapture, years before Jesus finally returns to usher in his millennial rule. If, as I believe, the Bible gives no such hope, but rather seeks to prepare us to endure and to overcome (two key words in the Book of Revelation) and to stand fast in our faith whatever comes, then such false teaching as this 'secret' rapture theory, may potentially be the cause of the great apostasy of which Jesus warns us in Matthew 24. How many who, on the basis of false teaching, believe that God has 'promised' that they will never have to go through the tribulation, will remain standing if they suddenly find themselves still on earth in those days, with that 'promise' in pieces at their feet?

I write as an evangelical, who believes the Bible is God's word, containing all that we need to find salvation in Jesus Christ, and explaining all truth to those who put their faith in him. This book therefore attempts to provide a biblical overview of the End-time message of the Book of Revelation, with particular reference to its setting within the context of the whole of Scripture. For this reason, I have not included the letters to the churches in chapters 2 and 3 in this book, but hope to look at them in a subsequent volume. Before you read this book, may I suggest that you read through the entire Book of Revelation, and that you keep it open before you as you read this one?

I am enormously grateful to the church family where I serve for their encouragement of my preaching ministry in general and of this project in particular. I also wish to thank my wife, Jackie, and our children, without whose love and attention this book would have been finished in half the time. I am particularly indebted to Helen Darvill, my former church secretary, a good friend, and mother to my youngest goddaughter, Phoebe, who painstakingly transcribed the original sermon tapes. Thanks also go to my publisher, Terra Nova, for taking the rough copy and transforming it into the book you now hold in your hands. Finally, as a preacher, I am grateful to countless other writers and preachers who have provided inspiration and material for my own thinking. Much of the credit for what is helpful in the following pages must go to those others, beginning with my parents, who introduced me to the wondrous world of biblical truth. If this book helps to guide you into just a little portion of that world, it will have served its purpose.

Paul Langham
June 2005

PART ONE

Introduction

1

WHY SHOULD WE READ THE BOOK OF REVELATION?

The future is both fascinating and terrifying, in more or less equal measure, to the people who inhabit planet earth in the early twenty-first century. Given the option, would you choose to know the date of your death? Would you choose to know what the future holds for you, your family and your loved ones? Or would you rather not know? Whatever your own response to those questions, attempting to unveil the future is big business. It has been reported that in the United Kingdom today, sixty percent of men and seventy percent of women read horoscopes regularly, despite the fact that repeated scientific studies continue to show that they are completely useless. Many are searching for knowledge of the future in spiritualistic, occult and 'new age' areas, and in the writings of false 'prophets'. In respectable academic fields too there is a tremendous drive to predict the future by scientific methods. Universities teach and undertake research in areas that include future prediction. There is even a new 'science' called Futurology, which means 'the study or prediction of future developments on the basis of existing conditions'. Many big businesses employ people specifically to predict the shape and demand of markets in the future. Yet it has been admitted by those working in some such fields that such 'scientific' prediction may enjoy a success rate no better than twenty-five percent.

Many predictions, whether stemming from academic or other sources, contribute to a very real climate of fear in our world today. At the end of the last century, there was a prediction that an asteroid was going to hit earth in the year 2038, wiping out all life. After a very short while, that prediction was withdrawn. And yet there is still fear, of many kinds. As a pastor, I observe fear permeating people's whole approach to life on a personal level: fear of illness; fear for their children; fear of losing work; fear of relational breakdown; fear of the consequences of personal debt; fear of fear itself. I am struck by the savage irony that – at least in the West – we enjoy the benefits of unparalleled material security, and yet are one of the most fearful generations ever to have lived. I believe that this is because our world, of itself, provides no firm ground for hope.

People are desperate for knowledge about the future and long for genuine hope for their own future. When you consider that deeply felt need in so many hearts, and the solid hope of a glorious eternity which Jesus Christ promises to all who follow and trust in him, it seems astonishing that the church is often silent about the future. The Bible tells us that the hope God offers us is an 'anchor for the soul' (see Hebrews 6:19). This true hope in God's promises should prevent us from drifting into danger, as an anchor does for a ship. So what exactly is that hope? I find that there is real confusion within the church about the answer to this question; so how can we expect anyone looking in from outside to be anything other than confused?

In a nutshell, the hope of the Christian is that, because of our faith in the saving death of Jesus Christ, we shall pass through death and live with him for ever. It is important to remember that when the Bible uses the word 'hope', it never uses it in the modern sense of 'something I'd really like but can't actually expect to happen'. The truth revealed in the Bible is that we can be 'sure of what we hope for and certain of what we do not see' (See Hebrews 11:1). But, sadly, many people in our churches today appear not truly to believe this. As for the majority of the population, who can blame them if they have the flimsiest knowledge of the Christian hope? Most people surveyed in the UK still claim to believe in life after death, but can only describe it in the most sentimental and insubstantial way. As a minister, I take many funerals of people who would have called themselves Christian, yet who enjoyed no assurance of eternal life. The most commonly expressed view of the bereaved people I seek to comfort is a vague, folk-religious belief that we become angels when we die, travel up some divine escalator and spend a rather unexciting eternity sitting on clouds, strumming harps. (I am convinced that a major cause for this is the Victorian hymn writers' discovery that 'love' rhymes with 'above'!) Alternatively, there is the belief that the deceased person is 'just around the corner', or in the sunlight or stars, close at hand, watching over their loved ones left here below. All that might sound comforting, but it is very far removed from the biblical hope. The Bible – and in particular the Book of Revelation – paints a picture which is richer, fuller and infinitely more desirable.

The irony of the church's silence about humankind's future appears the greater when we consider that the Bible is the most successful key to genuine prediction of the future the human race has ever known. God declared through the prophet Isaiah:

> I make known the end from the beginning,
> from ancient times, what is still to come.
> I say: My purpose will stand,
> and I will do all that I please.
>
> *Isaiah 46:10*

For two millennia, Christians have believed that the Bible is the word of the Lord, and the Bible is continually making predictions about the future. In fact, more than a quarter of all the verses in the Bible make some prediction about the future. In the New Testament alone, there are over three hundred references to the end of the world. Only Philemon and the third letter of John have no reference to the End times. Altogether, 737 separate predictions concerning the End are contained in the Scriptures. Of those, 594 (over 80%) have already come true; and all the others relate to the detail about the end of the world. The Bible has achieved 100% accuracy in predicting future events so far. So Christians really ought to be the best-placed people in the world not to worry about the future, but to actually know and trust what the Bible says about it.

Because our society at large does not believe this Christian hope, there are all sorts of negative consequences. The first is sheer folly. There are many examples of people who have been duped or misled by false 'revelations' into believing that the world will end on a particular date. Each has eventually realised what a waste of time it has all been. Folly can all too easily turn into tragedy. We are aware of mass suicides and massacres in various cults which promoted false apocalyptic expectation; and there will no doubt be more such disasters.

During the course of the twentieth century, the Western world moved from a climate of almost unlimited optimism to a mood of pervasive fear. If the key word at the beginning of the last century was 'progress' and the defining emotion hope – both of which were trampled in the mud and gore of the First World War – the key word at the beginning of the twenty-first century might well be 'survival', the defining emotion fear. We know all too much about what might happen: ecological disaster, asteroid collision, terrorist attack, biological warfare, chemical or nuclear accident.

The trouble is that in the church, too, there is uncertainty and error about what is going to happen. There is a great deal of confusion and uncertainty about the 'End'. Yet the Bible will yield its treasure to those who study it faithfully. But the Book of Revelation in particular has not been safely taught and, in many cases, not taught at all. When did you last hear a single sermon on Revelation in your church

– not counting chapters 2 & 3 – let alone a sermon series on the whole book? Misunderstanding is rife. It is amazing how many people have serious misconceptions concerning what the Bible says about heaven and about the return of Jesus. These issues, along with many other matters which need explanation, will be considered later in this book.

So why read Revelation? Why study the End times at all? I want to give you four reasons.

Because we are called to know the truth
When you become a Christian, you bow the knee before Jesus who *is* the truth. He promised his disciples that he would send them the Holy Spirit who would lead them into all truth. Jesus also promised that the truth will set you free. You are to be free to be the person God intended you to be from before the creation of the world. The truth about the end of planet earth is as much part of God's truth as any other part. The truth has power to give us freedom —from fear, from error, and from all the misguided individuals and organisations with their time charts, their predictions, their sales pitches and their false claims. A popular television show claims that the truth is 'out there'. Let me tell you, the reality is that *untruth* is out there in the world. So firstly, Christians are called to know the truth, for we are a people of the truth.

Because we are called to be prepared
Every so often, usually when the pressures of public ministry are weighing heavily upon me, I have a dream in which I enter a church service, either to lead or to preach, or to take a wedding or funeral, only to discover that I am totally unprepared. I am either dressed inappropriately or do not have my notes. We will all recall moments of sheer panic when we realised we were not prepared. If what I believe the Bible clearly foretells really is going to happen in the last days of planet earth, then you and I need to be prepared, in case those days come in our lifetime. Revelation is a call to endure, to persevere, to overcome. We cannot do that

if we do not know what to expect. I am not going to make any wild predictions. People who make predictions about when and where, and so on, are always wrong. They have to be, because Jesus taught us that they would be. Every generation has been tempted to think that it has sunk to the lowest ebb, that the End must be nigh because things are just so awful. The end of the first millennium saw a wealth of apocalyptic prediction, none of which came true. And at the turn of the second millennium, much of this fervour was whipped up again, and there have been many other times when events have convinced some that the End is near. So I will not make any predictions of that sort. However, logic does tell us that we are nearer the end now than any other generation before us has been, and each and every Christian needs to be prepared, in case the events described in the Book of Revelation unfold in our day.

Because we are people of 'the story'

Some stories are fictional; others are non-fiction! The Christian story is true. It is not man-made, nor is it mythological. Christians are people of real history, of the greatest true story ever told, including: a real creation; real people of faith; a real incarnation, God truly made man in the person of Jesus Christ; his real death on the cross; a bodily resurrection; a real outpouring of the Holy Spirit, and proclamation of the saving word of truth throughout the world.

Some people today share a view which was not uncommon in ancient Greek thought, that time is cyclical —that it just goes round and round, endlessly repeating over and over again. Jews and Christians have never held that belief. We believe that history, time, is linear. It goes from point A to point B; and as surely as it was begun by God, it will be ended by God.

I love a good story, especially crime thrillers. But imagine beginning a good novel at chapter three, or not bothering with the final chapter. One of the greatest ways of ruining a story is simply to pinch the beginning and the end – and that is what God's enemy, the devil, has been seeking to do for the last two hundred years. He has sought to rob the beginning of our story with the rise of evolutionism – which for many people today, especially in the scientific community has become a 'religious' position – and the attempted use of science to discredit Christian claims about God. This attack has been launched despite the fact that science resolutely refuses to be used in that way. This is not the field of this book, but it was fascinating to read recently that scientists at Massachusetts Institute of Technology using a computer model have 'discovered' that everyone on earth is descended from a single common ancestor, who lived in a village in eastern Asia in the year 1,415 BC (around 3,500 years ago). In the 1990s, mathematicians in Cambridge, collaborating with colleagues around the world, began feeding huge computers with the data necessary to predict the likelihood of life beginning by chance. When the number came out, it was enormous: 10 to the power of 40. It is a number too great to comprehend. One way to visualise it would be to imagine covering a land mass the size of Russia with 5p coins, up to the height of the moon. Then, take another 1000 land masses the same size as Russia and do exactly the same, covering them with 5p coins up to the moon. What I did not tell you was that one of those 5p coins is painted red, and you have to find it. Your chances of finding that one coin in amongst all those others are similar to the chances that life began by accident. Where do you read that in the press? It is in the scientific press, but does not get headlines in the national media.

We have all heard about the Big Bang theory. We are told that it is a modern theory. One scholar put it like this: 'At the briefest moment in time after creation, all the matter of the universe was concentrated in a tiny space, no larger than a grain of mustard'. Can you guess who said that? Einstein, perhaps? Or Hawking? In fact it was written by a thirteenth century theologian in a commentary on the Book of Genesis! It seems that whenever scientists clamber up yet another supposedly undiscovered peak of human knowledge, they find a group of theologians sitting on the top waiting for them.

The Christian community today is in desperate need of recovering the truth concerning the beginning and the end of the true story God has revealed to us. If we leave out the beginning and the end, then we are missing something vital in God's revelation; and our world today needs, more than anything else, the true, *full* story.

Because of a promise and a warning

The fourth reason is the simplest and, quite possibly, the most challenging. We read the Book of Revelation because it is the only book in Scripture that promises a blessing on those who read it, hear it and take it to heart (see 1:3), and a curse on those who add words to it or take them away from it (22:18f). I would like to encourage you to read the Book of Revelation in one sitting before you read any more chapters of this book. It will only take you as long as watching a television soap opera, but it will do you far more good!

Heavenly Father, in your word you assure me that my hope as a Christian is to be an anchor for my soul, firm and secure. Please help me to walk in this hope, in Jesus' name. Amen.

2

HOW SHOULD WE READ THE BOOK OF REVELATION?

It may be that the previous chapter has convinced you of the value of reading the Book of Revelation, but you may now be daunted at the prospect and wondering how to do so. For far too long – for much of Christian history in fact – the Book of Revelation has been ignored. People have thought it just too perplexing, full of confusing picture language: dragons, beasts, horns, stars, angels, trumpets, seals. Many cannot even be bothered to begin. Here are four guidelines to bear in mind as we read the Book of Revelation.

The Book of Revelation is unique in style and origin

Can you imagine the Bible without Revelation? Can you imagine the New Testament – the whole canon of Scripture – ending with the letter of Jude? Jude is one of the two shortest epistles in the New Testament, twenty or so verses, written to a tiny church which was rapidly draining of its character, creed and converts. Even if we are poorly acquainted with Revelation, we are grateful that it is there. But we must recognise that the Book of Revelation is not only different from all the other New Testament books in style, but it is also unique in origin. All the other books of the New Testament were intended to be written, and then planned. Think of the way Luke begins his Gospel, by making the reader aware of how much research he has put into it. Marvel at the way in which Paul crafts the flow of his arguments in Galatians or Romans. That is not in any way to discount the inspiring work of the Holy Spirit, which is the hallmark of all Scripture, as the Lord guides the human authors of his word while at the same time using their human abilities. But the difference with Revelation is striking. John had no intention of writing this book. It came upon him, without any warning, in a series of visions. Note, as you read it through, the number of times the Spirit says to him, "Write." Imagine seeing an amazing vision and someone saying, "Get it all down on paper." This explains why the Greek is not as polished as in John's Gospel and letters. John is only the scribe. The real author is God himself.

It should not divide us from other Christians

Secondly, as we read the Book of Revelation, we should be determined not to allow different views on any issues to divide us from other Christians. We still worship the same Lord, however we feel the End times are going to work out.

We need to understand the meaning and nature of 'apocalyptic' literature

Do not worry about some of the unusual words we shall be meeting. The modern mind encountering the word 'apocalyptic' imagines wild, exotic writing, full of strange language, often arcanely expressed, doom-laden and difficult to understand. Yet the Greek word 'apocalypse' actually means 'unveiling' —'revelation'. In other words, the Book of Revelation is intended to make things clear! Things are revealed, not obscured. That should encourage us as we begin. God's intention in inspiring the Book of Revelation is to take us from the small stage of human history, where everything is turmoil and chaos, and, as he hitches up the backdrop of the set, to reveal to us things which lie beyond the scene of history. Here are two things which no human historian can write about: what is happening in heaven, and what will happen in earth's future. But when God writes history, he gives the total picture, because God not only observes the world's events, he orders them. Everything – past, present, future – is held together by God as Creator. 'Apocalyptic' simply means history written from God's point of view, which offers us an understanding of world events in the light of what God is doing.

We need to understand the pattern and presentation of apocalyptic writing

(i) Pattern

The pattern of apocalyptic writing is essentially moral. You and I look at the world and, so often, we see chaos, unfairness, injustice. We see things happening that never should happen (whether natural disasters, or the cruelties inflicted by human beings), and we cry out, 'Why?' I find one of the wonderful characteristics of the Bible is that it is honest enough to record the bewilderment of some of our fellow travellers on this human journey through life —Job, King David. All cried out their 'Why?' to heaven, as Jesus did on the cross. The Book of Revelation is written partly to deal with that great question on so many lips, to show that God is in control and one day will bring everything to a wonderful, just and fair conclusion.

(ii) Presentation

The presentation of apocalyptic writing is often symbolic. We assume we will be confused, as if symbols are foreign to our minds. Yet we use symbols all the time. Think of a teacher explaining a new concept to a class of children — 'Well, it's like this....' Think how often Jesus, when talking about the kingdom, said, 'The kingdom of heaven is like....' We use symbolism – word pictures – all the time. Picturing helps us to imagine. That is why, when we explain a difficult concept to people, the response is often, 'Oh, I *see* what you mean.' That is why Revelation is full of 'word pictures', language which helps us to visualise and to understand what otherwise would be incomprehensible. The symbols of Revelation are intended to help, not to hinder. Too often, the symbolism has put people off. But it is really quite simple. The symbols come in only four categories.

- Some are obvious in meaning. The 'dragon' and 'the serpent', for instance, clearly refer to the devil; we know this because it is made clear elsewhere in Scripture.
- Secondly, some terms are explained in context. For example, when we read in chapter one about the stars, the Spirit actually explains to John that they represent angels.
- Thirdly, some have parallels or are explained elsewhere in Scripture, particularly in the Old Testament —symbols like the rainbow, the rod of iron, the morning star, and so on.
- Finally, some symbols are obscure —but very few. What the white stone of Revelation 2:17 means, nobody knows. I suspect we will not know until we receive one.

Numbers are also used as symbols. You will find that numbers occur more in Revelation than anywhere else in the New Testament.

(i) 'One' refers to exclusiveness, primacy, excellence. Jesus says of himself, "I am the First and the Last. I am the Living One..." (1:17).

(ii) 'Four' speaks of the completeness of the whole of the created order. You will read about the four corners of the earth, the four winds, the four angels standing at the corners of the earth.

(iii) 'Six' is imperfection, man's number —always one less than perfection.

(iv) 'Seven' is fullness, perfection, totality — 'the seven spirits before his throne' (see 1:4), the seven lampstands, the seven churches, and so on.

(v) 'Twelve' refers to God's people: the twelve tribes of Israel, the twelve apostles. Often, composites are used: the 'twenty-four' elders of 4:4 bring both Israel and apostles together, the universality of God's redeemed people in Christ.

(vi) 'Thousand' represents a large number, a multitude, or a very long period of time.

WAYS OF INTERPRETING OR READING THE BOOK OF REVELATION

During Christian history, the Book of Revelation has been interpreted in four main ways. Please do not worry if you cannot remember the words used to describe them.

(i) Preterist

This approach claims that all the predictions contained within the Book of Revelation were fulfilled during the days of the Roman Empire. The strength of this approach is that it begins – as Bible study always should – with the original context. The major weakness is that it renders Revelation absolutely irrelevant to us today. This strikes a blow against the orthodox Christian belief that all Scripture is both the inspired word of God and continually relevant in every age. (See 2 Timothy 3:16.) The other great weakness is that so many of the things predicted in the Book of Revelation quite clearly did not happen in the days of the Roman Empire. At least, no one that I know has ever claimed to be living in the new Jerusalem!

(ii) Historicist

This approach seeks to fit the predictions of Revelation – sometimes over and over again – into every period of earth history between Christ's first coming and his second. This is the method which produces all those astonishing timescales and charts. One scholar even indexed the Book of Revelation to the Cambridge University Encyclopaedia of World History. This is the school of thought that tries to tell you who precisely 666 is. Supposedly it was Genghis, it was Hitler, it was Stalin, it was Saddam, and so on....

(iii) Futurist

As the term suggests, a futurist holds that all the predictions refer to the very last few days of earth history. This is the approach which lies behind the *Left Behind* series of novels, which have sold in their millions across the world.

(iv) Idealist

This is a typically modern, liberal idea —rooted in the post-enlightenment belief that no one writing in one specific time can accurately predict events in another, future, time. In this view, all the predictions of the Book of Revelation are purely figurative, and should be seen as providing spiritual encouragement in times of ordinary, human tribulation.

Not surprisingly, I am clear that the fourth view is unworthy of Scripture and must be rejected. I believe that all the first three have merit and are useful —especially when held together. I call this the combined approach. Its strength lies in its ability to acknowledge that:

- The Book of Revelation clearly had very definite things to say to the first generation of Christians undergoing the horrors of early Roman persecution.
- It has had much to say about the whole history of the Christian era, and continues to speak to us today.
- There yet remains an ultimate fulfilment of much of what we read in its pages, to which we look forward, and in hope of which we join our voices with John's own: 'Even so, come Lord Jesus.'

The advantage of such an approach is demonstrated by a quick look at perhaps the most familiar 'character' in the Book of Revelation, namely the 'beast' of chapter 13. If we adopt the Preterist approach on its own, we have to conclude that, whatever or whoever the beast may have been, its days are long since over, and we do not have to concern ourselves with its identity. If we follow the Historicist approach, we find ourselves constantly attempting to locate the individual or system in world history. Is it Genghis Khan or Pol Pot? Nazism or Stalinism? We will almost certainly choose the one which seems to be oppressing us at this moment in time. I remember, a number of years ago, reading an article in a Christian magazine, which sought to identify the beast as the European Union, on the grounds that the beast in Revelation has ten horns, then the number of member states. As soon as the EU enlarged, the analogy collapsed.

If, however, we agree that all three approaches reveal different facets of the truth, we find ourselves on much firmer ground. We can acknowledge that the Roman Empire – or even the emperor himself – was the initial manifestation of the beast, for John and his readers. But we can also acknowledge that there have been many, many 'beasts' throughout history – before and since John received his visions – and that these 'beasts', whether individuals or systems, will continue as long as human society endures. Yet again, we can be on our guard for the ultimate manifestation of ungodly power, as the days of earth draw to a close.

When or why?

Having suggested that we interpret the Book of Revelation through a combination of the three methods mentioned above, we must note that all three share a major flaw, one which emerges in all the more excitable books on the topic of the End times. This is the assumption that Revelation's key question is 'When?' —in other words, that Revelation was written in order to help us understand times and dates, so that we might be able to predict when Jesus will return. But in fact the Bible's apocalypses or unveilings never have the question 'When?' as the primary issue. The primary question is always 'Why?' *Why* was this revealed to John? *Why* was John told to write it down? *Why* are we told to read it and to keep it? *Why* was Revelation written?

It seems to me that the key to understanding apocalyptic or predictive literature, in Christian Scripture, is this: the future is only ever unveiled in order that it might influence the present. In other words, we are told what will happen

THEN in order that it might change the way we live NOW. I believe that will happen to you as you faithfully study the Book of Revelation. It will change you, without a doubt. You will not emerge with a perfectly clear schematic for the end of the world, but you will emerge with the confidence that, whatever mess the world in general or your life in particular seems to be in at the moment, God is in control, on his throne, and that history is moving inexorably to the day appointed by him for the consummation of the human story and the renewal of the cosmos. With that insight, you will not be able to live in the way that you now live.

A very good example of this key to understanding predictive Scripture occurs in 2 Peter 3. In verse 10, Peter unveils the future end of planet earth to his readers: 'The heavens will disappear with a roar; the elements will be destroyed by fire, and the earth and everything in it will be laid bare.' Then, in verse 11, he gives the reason for this unveiling of the future – 'Since everything will be destroyed in this way, what kind of people ought you to be? You ought to live holy and godly lives, as you look forward to the day of God and speed its coming'. 'Why?' —that is the key question.

The Book of Revelation was written to reveal things. It was written to ordinary people. Do remember that. Think what Paul said in 1 Corinthians 1:26.

Brothers, think of what you were when you were called. Not many of you were wise by human standards; not many were influential; not many were of noble birth.

Not many in the early church were wise, by human standards, yet these are the people to whom the Book of Revelation was written. It was not written for university professors, nor for theologians; and yet, sadly, there is a widespread notion – maybe you share it – that Revelation simply cannot be understood. It is just too difficult, too complicated, too bizarre. And yet, Revelation, along with the rest of Scripture, will yield its treasure to you if you approach it with a faithful and obedient heart.

Common sense is a basic requirement. We should not take the whole book literally, and neither should we take it all symbolically. We need to understand the difference between literal and symbolic. Croatian is not a difficult language. A three-year old Croatian child can speak it quite happily, but it is difficult for you and me because we have not learnt it. We can understand the language of Revelation, if we are willing to apply ourselves so that it becomes familiar. We are quite used to differentiating different types of language. Let me demonstrate this: 'The stars will fall from heaven, the sun will cease to shine, the moon will be turned to blood, fire will rain from heaven and the earth and everything in it will be laid bare — the rest of the country will have sunny intervals and scattered showers.' We are quite accustomed to distinguishing between different types of writing and speaking. We understand, from the way people write or speak, the weight that is attached to what is said. Much writing in Revelation and in other parts of the Bible depends on our understanding of context. You and I all know what an 'armchair sportsman' is. But if you try to explain it to someone who is learning the English language, you have a whole lot of contextualisation to do. So, for example, in Revelation, we can see that the four horsemen of the Apocalypse are symbolic, but that the death, war, famine, and disease they bring are literal.

A manual for persecuted Christians

It seems to me that the primary purpose was to prepare John's readers – then and now – for what was and is coming. The answer is actually in Revelation 1:9f. 'I, John, your brother and companion in the suffering and kingdom and patient endurance that are ours in Jesus, was on the island of Patmos because of the word of God and the testimony of Jesus.' John was a prisoner because persecution was already happening. His exclusive devotion to Jesus Christ was treason in the Roman world where many gods were worshipped, including the emperor, and all had to be worshipped equally. Julius Caesar was the first to declare himself divine; Augustus the first to build temples in his honour; Nero the first to begin persecuting Christians because they would not bow the knee. One of Nero's ideas of fun was to tie Christians up, and then pour pitch over them before setting them on fire as human torches for his garden parties. Domitian, who followed Nero a few years later, began a widespread persecution of the Christian church which lasted for two hundred years. He decreed that, once a year on a special day, incense was to be burnt to him on his day, and that day was called the Lord's Day – and that is the day on which Revelation began (1:10). When we read, 'On the Lord's Day I was in the Spirit', most of us think John means what we call 'Sunday'. But the early church simply called it 'the first day of the week'. (See Acts 20:7.) The 'Lord's Day' is a direct reference to the day when the whole of the then known world had to worship Domitian as lord and god; and it was on that very day that John's world was invaded by this revelation that the one true God was sovereign. This must have been hugely significant both for John and those churches for whom this letter would be smuggled off Patmos. Tough times lay ahead for the church. Confession of Jesus Christ was going to become a matter of life and death. John's was an age in which the Greek word for witness, martyr, was about to acquire a new, grim meaning. John, at this stage in his life, was probably the only one of the twelve apostles who had not been martyred for his faith. We do well to remember that for countless numbers of our brother and sister Christians around the world, their confession still is a matter of life and death. And it may become so even in the West.

So, in many senses, Revelation is a manual for martyrdom. In 2:10ff we are called to be faithful, even to the point of death. John exalts us to two states of mind, one passive, the other active. We are to endure and we are to overcome. In many ways, the key verse in the whole book is 14:12, where John writes, 'This calls for patient endurance on the part of the saints....' The word 'overcome' occurs many times throughout the book. Each of the seven letters to the churches ends with Jesus promising a reward to those who overcome. Beyond the symbolism of each reward is the glorious prospect of eternity spent in the presence of God himself.

Yet the Book of Revelation does not encourage in us a complacent approach to the certainty of Christ's return to the earth. The book contains some very strong indications that the way we live now, and the state of our hearts and minds when Jesus returns, really matters. Those who have been faithful, those who have endured and persevered, those who have overcome, will inherit the crown of life; but those who have disowned, who have deliberately gone away and refused to be faithful will be erased. One of the promises to the person who overcomes, in Revelation 3:5, is that, 'I will never blot out his name from the book of life....' The Greek refers to the scraping clean of the parchment – the way they recycled parchment in the ancient world, scraping it off with a knife. The rest of the New Testament tells a similar story. The manual for discipleship that we have in Matthew's Gospel contains most of Jesus' teaching on hell – and it is written to Christians: 'But whoever disowns me before men, I will disown him before my Father in heaven', says Jesus. (Matthew 10:33). Matthew 24 and 25, which we will be looking at in a future chapter, particularly warns that 'unfaithful servants will be given a place with the unbelievers'; and Paul writes,

> If we disown him,
> he will also disown us....
>
> *2 Timothy 2:11b*

Better theologians than I have debated whether it is possible for someone, having once become a Christian, to then lose their eternal life. (See R T Kendall's *Once Saved, Always Saved* and David Pawson's *Once Saved, Always Saved?*). The preacher and pastor in me simply wants to encourage you to make sure there is absolutely no chance of that at all, by standing firm in your faith and looking forward to the Day of the Lord. One thing I have learnt in my pastoral ministry is that Christians who worry that they might have lost their salvation give ample evidence by their very anxiety that they have not.

So Revelation is written to give us a hope for the future and to call us to be faithful in pursuing that hope, even in the face of pressure and persecution and death. We live in a world of much despair; a world that is without hope for the many who do not know God. Christians should be beacons of hope, because in the Scriptures we have a reliable account of what has occurred, what is now occurring and what is yet to come. We understand that one day the Lord will return; that he will set up his rule of righteousness over the nations, and all will bow to him. This hope, according to the writer to the Hebrews, is an anchor for the soul, firm and secure. It is my prayer that this guide will help you to get your anchor down now.

Heavenly Father, thank you for your word. I am sorry for the times I have taken it for granted, neglecting its fulsome teaching on what will happen to the world in which I live. But, Lord, I say to you today that I want to learn, I want to understand, I want to know, in order that I may hold firm the faith you have set before me; that I may be one who perseveres and endures and overcomes, and that I may shine as a beacon of hope in a world that has lost its way. Lord, give me that anchor, I pray, as I read your written word. Make my soul firm and secure in this great hope; and, Lord, help me to live a godly life, enduring all things with patience, and let me look forward to the day when you return. Even so, come Lord Jesus. Amen.

PART TWO

The Scriptural Context

3

WHAT DOES THE OLD TESTAMENT SAY ABOUT THE END TIMES?

In order to gain a comprehensive picture of a large or complicated object – a city, say, or the site of an air crash – it is often necessary to gain height and distance to enable the site to be seen, approaching it from several different angles and viewpoints. A helicopter is ideal for the purpose; and in this chapter we are going to take a helicopter ride, in order to see this large, complex word of the Lord to us through John, by God's Spirit, from some different viewpoints. If it sometimes seems as if we are turning our backs on Revelation and flying in the opposite direction, it is with the sole purpose that we should be in a good position to turn round, look at and read Revelation with fuller understanding.

Gaining this aerial view will mean looking at those parts of the Old Testament that are relevant to this study. Why? There are a number of important reasons.

First of all, the Old Testament is the word of God as surely as is the New Testament. Peter, one of Jesus' right hand men, taught that prophecy never originated in the minds of men, but that the prophets spoke by the Spirit of the Lord. Jesus constantly referred to the Old Testament, thereby affirming its authority. Following his resurrection, on the evening of that day, Jesus joined Cleopas and another disciple on the Emmaus road, and, in order to explain the crucifixion, the resurrection and all that was taking place, he used the Old Testament. Too many Christians today ignore the Old Testament as being simply a book of Jewish writings; yet it is vital for the Christian. So much of Christian truth is foreshadowed in the pages of the Old Testament. Just think of Abraham and Isaac and the sacrifice on Moriah —the provision of the ram for sacrifice foreshadowing the gift of the only Son. The Exodus, the Passover, the flight from Egypt, the crossing of the Red Sea —are all symbols of what was to be fully revealed in the life and death of Jesus Christ. And less well-known, even by Christians who read it, the Old Testament has a great deal to say about the End.

Secondly, there is an important principle: we interpret Scripture by Scripture. We use passages of the Bible to shed light on, interpret and enlarge upon other passages. Think of the four Gospels for example. Perhaps John is your favourite Gospel, because that has the densest theological working of the story of Jesus; but you would not for a moment want to be without the beginning of Matthew and Luke, which give you the nativity stories, and much other material. A classic example in the theology of the End times is the whole question of the rapture of the saints, which is not explicitly mentioned in Revelation at all —so we need to look elsewhere in the New Testament to find Paul spelling out exactly what is going to happen.

Thirdly, the more complete our view, the more accurate it will be. I remember an early advertisement for a national daily newspaper which was launched a few years ago. It began with a close-up shot of a banker, very smartly dressed, walking down a city street, briefcase strapped to his wrist. As the camera pulled back, it revealed a skinhead running at him, inviting the obvious conclusion that the skinhead was about to rob the banker. The shot pulled back further, this time to show masonry falling from a building above. The final shot showed the skinhead diving to push the banker out of harm's way. The more complete your view, the more accurate your view. I have already proposed that the End time scenario provides one of the greatest potential areas for error in Christian teaching today, and we need to guard against error. Jesus taught that one of the signs of the End will be a deception among the elect —so we need to grasp as much of the breadth of the teaching of Scripture as we can.

Fourthly, the Author of Scripture is consistent. What God clearly says in one place, he will not contradict in another —this is a principle of studying the Scriptures. So we ought to expect to find the voice of the Old Testament speaking in the same voice as John. It is a great encouragement to us when that is, indeed, what we find. Finally, the Book of Revelation itself is steeped in the Old Testament. Although the Book of Revelation never once directly quotes the Old Testament, there are 676 references —either verbal allusions to, or parallels with, the Old Testament. Of these, 53 are from Exodus, 99 from Psalms, 128 from Isaiah, 92 from Ezekiel and 82 from Daniel.

HOW SHOULD WE HANDLE OLD TESTAMENT PROPHECY?

What do we expect when we read prophecy? We have already seen the need to distinguish between different types of writing, and we need to understand the characteristics of the style of writing, if we are to understand it.

1. Biblical prophecy is sometimes capable of multiple fulfilment.

A single prophecy can find partial fulfilment again and again, and yet still point to an ultimate End time fulfilment. Think of the prophecy of Joel, 'I will pour out my Spirit upon all flesh' —a partial fulfilment on the day of Pentecost; partial fulfilments each time people are filled with the Spirit and converted to Christ; and yet also looking ahead to that great Day when the earth will be full of God's Spirit in a way that it cannot be until Christ returns. Or think of the way that the Old Testament uses the image of the beast – in Daniel in particular – to symbolise governments, individuals, or institutions that oppress believers. Every age has its tyrants and oppressors of God's people, and each age, therefore, brings partial fulfilment of what is foreseen. Yet, in the Book of Revelation, we are pointed toward a final fulfilment in the End time beast, the antichrist. This is confirmed in the New Testament. When John writes of the antichrist, he teaches that many antichrists are already abroad —partial fulfilment pointing towards a final fulfilment.

2. Biblical prophecy can sometimes have a 'concertina' effect.

I grew up in the Lake District, and could see the Langdale peaks from my bedroom window. From that distance, they all seemed to be stacked one against the other. You could not see the valleys and the land that lies between them. A similar 'concertina' effect can be seen in many of the Old Testament prophecies which speak of the return from exile of the people of Israel, and yet then immediately skip ahead and look towards the End times. This is seen as well in Jesus' reply in Matthew 24 (which we will be considering in depth in the next chapter) when the disciples ask him specifically about the destruction of the temple. In his reply he interweaves his prediction of the destruction of the temple – which took place some forty years later – but then goes on to teach them about the End times.

3. Sometimes, contrasting prophecies are given about the same event.

It is a way that the Bible writers have, under the inspiration of God's Spirit, of giving us different perspectives on the same event or idea. A very good example, in our present study, is 'the day of the Lord'. One prophet will emphasise that the day of the Lord comes to give blessing; while another, Jeremiah particularly, will always emphasise that the day of the Lord is for judgment. Isaiah, the greatest of all the prophets, never mentions the day of the Lord without holding those two in tension. In the New Testament, in his letters to the Thessalonians, Paul gives two different perspectives on the rapture – discussing in one how it will affect believers, and in the other how it will affect those who are to be judged as unbelievers.

4. We must understand that biblical prophecy is never given without purpose.

The technical way of saying this is that prophecy is teleological. God's unveiling of the future is never given simply as an end in itself, but always to transform the present. If what God unveils to us about the future does not transform the way we live now, then it is not doing its job. When you read the Book of Revelation – and I hope that if you have not already read it as a whole, in one go, as part of your study using this book, you will do so now – your life will be changed. You will not be able to remain the same in the present, because your mind has been opened to the future.

5. Finally, biblical prophecy is Christ-centred.

The words uttered by the prophets were full of Jesus. The first and second comings are woven into the very fabric of the Old Testament. Just think of those Christmas readings: 'The virgin will be with child...' (Isaiah 7:14); 'But you, Bethlehem Ephrathah...' (Micah 5:2). None of this should come as a surprise. The One who is Alpha and Omega, the One who began time and creation, the One who will wrap time and creation up, is bound to pervade the pages of the prophets, bound to take centre stage in the writings of God's people. He is both the agent of creation and the means by which all things will be consummated and transformed.

SO WHAT DOES THE OLD TESTAMENT SAY ABOUT THE END TIMES?

1. A created order in which he can share intimacy with his people remains God's ideal

We do well to start right at the beginning with Genesis chapters 1 and 2. In his love and mercy, God decided to share the 'community life' of his own nature – three persons in one God – and he created our world. In it he planted a 'garden of delight', as the dwelling place of our first ancestors. Everything in those early pages of the Bible suggests that he was more than a little pleased with the work of his hands —it was good. After Adam and Eve's fall from grace, the whole created order needed to be redeemed, but there is no hint in Scripture that creation as a principle will ever be replaced in God's plans. We can expect, then, a created eternity —unless the Scriptures tell us otherwise. Why did God create us? What was his purpose, his design and his heart's desire? It was to share the intimacy of his 'rest' with us. The six phases or periods of creation are all defined by the phrase, 'And there was evening, and there was morning —the ...th day.' But not the 7th —that has no end in sight. Paradise on earth was God's gift to men and women —his heart's desire to share intimacy with us. I find one of the most moving passages of Scripture to be the description of God's habit of walking in the garden 'in the cool of the day'. And one of the most poignant passages follows immediately, when we hear God's anguished cry, 'Where are you?' as he realises that his beloved creatures are hiding from him. As Lesslie Newbigin comments, the rest of Scripture can be seen as the story of God's attempts to recover his intimacy with the creatures who have flown from him into sin. Hence the significance of the concept of 'rest' in the Old Testament —the promised land will be a place of rest, peace and plenty. This theme is picked up by the author of the letter to the Hebrews. The passage from 3:7 to 4:11 is an extended commentary on Psalm 95, itself a reflection on the sin which caused the first generation of God's people after the Exodus to be excluded from the 'land of rest'. Psalm 95 ends with the judgment of God, "They shall never enter my rest." The author of Hebrews develops this theme to show that God still desires to invite people to enter his rest, which we can know in part now, but which we shall inherit ultimately at the end of all things.

God's desire for intimacy is also revealed throughout the Old Testament in the phrase which first occurs in Exodus 6:7 as 'I will take you as my own people, and I will be your God.' This phrase occurs many more times in Scripture, and finds ultimate fulfilment in the revelation of the new Jerusalem, descending from heaven, with the words, "Now the dwelling of God is with men, and he will live with them. They will be his people, and God himself will be with them and be their God" (Revelation 21:3).

From Genesis 12, when God makes his covenant with Abraham, 'the land' (specifically the land of Israel) becomes a pivotal feature of the Old Testament. The people of God are regularly defined by their relationship to the land. Remember the Lord's promise to Joshua, as he prepared to lead God's people back into the promised land: "I will give you every place where you set your foot, as I promised Moses" (Joshua 1:3b). Loss of the land is one of the greatest calamities that can befall God's people. And notice that when Jesus declares that the meek are blessed, he promises that they will inherit the earth.

2. There will come a day when the Lord will establish his rule of righteousness and justice in the present-world order

This is often seen in the Old Testament as the everlasting kingdom of David. Genesis 49:10 speaks of a coming day when all nations will give God obedience. When is that day? How is that going to happen? How is the Lord going to achieve the working out of that promise? 2 Samuel 7:16 holds out the promise of an everlasting kingdom for David. How is this to come about? How will this be fulfilled? Of course, this promise was partially fulfilled in the birth of Jesus, in the rule of Jesus and in Jesus' teaching on the kingdom —but his time on earth was fairly short. Where is the kingdom today? We cannot claim it is perfectly here in the church. So where is this everlasting kingdom which was prophesied? To what extent is God's kingdom present in your life, in my life?

So many other books in the Old Testament are highly significant in relation to the Book of Revelation. Exodus is the first to mention the 'book of life' – and how significant the book of life is to the later prophets such as Daniel as well as the author of Revelation. In Numbers we meet the first occurrence of the phrase 'at the end of days'; 'in the latter days'. Psalm 72 is another good example of the way that biblical prophecy is capable of multiple fulfilment. Written in the first instance about an earthly king (probably Solomon), it also looks ahead to the coming of the Messiah, and to his second coming. In v. 8, the worldwide dominion of God upon the earth is foreseen. In Psalm 96 the Lord is seen coming to judge the earth and its peoples 'in righteousness and truth'. So we are encouraged to look for the one who is coming, for the judge who is approaching —coming where? He is coming to earth for judgment. Isaiah chapter 2 speaks of 'the last days'; it predicts the pre-eminence of Jerusalem, the nations streaming into it. Then, 'He will judge between the nations and will settle disputes for many peoples. They will beat their swords into ploughshares and their spears into pruning hooks' (Isaiah 2:4a).

One of the things we are looking for in the rule of Christ upon earth is universal disarmament, a period of international peace. Consider the language of verses 10, 19 and 21, 'Go into the rocks, hide in the ground from dread of the LORD and the splendour of his majesty... Men will flee to caves in the rocks and to holes in the ground from the dread of the LORD.... They will flee to caverns in the rocks...', with the language of Revelation 6:15–17, 'Then the kings of the earth, the princes, the generals, the rich, the mighty, and every slave and every free man hid in caves and among the rocks of the mountains.' Isaiah saw it all, eight hundred years before Jesus was born.

Again in Isaiah 11 we see a prophetic combination of Christ's first and second comings. Verses 1–3 are easily applied to the earthly life of Jesus Christ, but verses 4 and 5 introduce a theme of global judgment which we will not see until he returns. In verse 4 we read that, 'He will strike the earth with the rod of his mouth....' Here, Isaiah is describing the rider of Revelation 19:15. Again, Isaiah emphasises that Christ's End time rule will affect the very nature of the created world. Nature, now red in tooth and claw, will be transformed. Consider Isaiah 11:6–8, 'The wolf will live with the lamb, the leopard will lie down with the goat, the calf and the lion and the yearling together; and a little child will lead them. The cow will feed with the bear, their young will lie down together, and the lion will eat straw like the ox. The infant will play near the hole of the cobra, and the young child put his hand into the viper's nest. They will neither harm nor destroy on all my holy mountain, for the earth will be full of the knowledge of the LORD as the waters cover the sea.' These ideas are echoed in Isaiah 65:25, too. And notice: here it is not heaven that is going to be filled with the knowledge of God, it is the earth. The prophets are quite insistent that we take this to heart. In Habakkuk 2:14 we have, again, the phrase '...the earth will be filled with the knowledge of the glory of the LORD, as the waters cover the sea.' Not the heavens, not somewhere out of time, but here, the earth, will be filled with knowledge of God's glory. I hope that the Old Testament is persuading you of the fact that there will come a day when this earth will be filled with God's glory.

3. The Old Testament also makes it clear that the present created order – both heavens and earth – will be renewed

In Isaiah 34, in which the Lord pronounces judgment on the nations, verse 4 leaps off the page: 'All the stars of the heavens will be dissolved, and the sky rolled up like a scroll; all the starry host will fall.... like shrivelled figs from the fig-tree.' In Matthew 24, that is exactly the language that Jesus uses to teach his disciples how to read the signs.

Perhaps the most astonishing passage in the whole of Isaiah with regard to the End times (again recalling that he wrote eight centuries before Jesus was born) comes in 65:17. 'Behold, I will create new heavens and a new earth. The former things will not be remembered, nor will they come to mind.... I will create Jerusalem to be a delight... the sound of weeping and of crying will be heard in it no more.' What does John record in Revelation 21:1–4, when he sees Jerusalem, the holy city, coming down prepared as a bride to the earth? He sees new heavens and a new earth. And what does he say will be a characteristic of this new Jerusalem, where saved human beings and God will dwell together? He says there will be no more tears, no more crying —exactly the same language as we find in Isaiah.

4. The Lord will appear physically on the earth at the end of days

In the midst of Job's torment and pain and agony, there is suddenly almost a searing light, when he says,

> I know that my Redeemer lives,
> and that in the end he will stand upon the earth.
> And after my skin has been destroyed,
> yet in my flesh I will see God;
> I myself will see him
> with my own eyes — I, and not another.
> How my heart yearns within me!
>
> *Job 19:25ff*

With our Greek-influenced world-view, most people in the West who believe in an afterlife think that our ultimate destiny is a sort of elevator ride of the spirit into the great beyond, where, if we do anything at all, we will sit on clouds and play our harps. That is not what the Bible promises. The hope of an earthly resurrection, the physical return of the Lord, is far more at the heart of the Jewish-Christian understanding than the later Greek world-view. Job says, 'My heart yearns within me.' Does your heart yearn within you for that day when Christ will once again stand on this earth? In Psalm 16:9f., David writes, "...my body also will rest secure, because you will not abandon me to the grave, nor will you let your Holy One see decay." Notice again how 'earthy' the Christian faith is. There is nothing insubstantial about the Hebrew and Christian hope. It is physical, it is solid, it is real, it is created. The ultimate distinction in the universe is between Creator and creation, and that distinction will remain. Peter quoted this same verse on the day of Pentecost, recorded in Acts 2, showing how it was fulfilled through David, through Christ and on into the believer. Think, too, of Paul's teaching in 1 Corinthians 15, about the new 'imperishable' body which is central to the Christian's hope.

5. The Old Testament points to a day of final judgment.

I thought in my heart,

> "God will bring to judgment
> both the righteous and the wicked...."
> *Ecclesiastes 3:17a*

In Isaiah 45:23, we read that every knee will bow before the Lord. When do we look for that day? When is it coming? Paul confidently predicted, in Philippians 2:10f, that,

> ...at the name of Jesus every knee should bow,
> in heaven and on earth and under the earth,
> and every tongue confess that Jesus Christ is Lord,
> to the glory of God the Father.

And at the very end of the Old Testament, in Malachi 4, the final prophet sees the day of the Lord as a day of blessing and of judgment.

When Jesus began his public ministry, he took as his

manifesto the opening verses of Isaiah 61, quoted in Luke chapter 4,

> The Spirit of the Lord is on me,
> because he has anointed me
> to preach good news to the poor.
> He has sent me to proclaim freedom for the prisoners
> and recovery of sight for the blind,
> to release the oppressed,
> to proclaim the year of the Lord's favour.
>
> *Luke 4:18f.*

The fascinating thing to notice is that Jesus stops mid-verse in his quotation from Isaiah. He omits Isaiah's final words, 'the day of vengeance of our God'. Once again, we see in Isaiah the 'concertina' effect of prophecy. The year of the Lord's favour refers to the earthly ministry of Christ and the whole period of earth history since. Jesus is announcing that he has come as Messiah to bring people to faith, to show abroad God's love, to offer everyone salvation, not to condemn. The day of vengeance is yet stored for that final and terrible day when Christ will return, as Lord and Judge of all.

Isaiah 56 talks of the salvation of 'foreigners who bind themselves to the LORD'. When the Lord established his covenant with Abraham, he promised that all peoples would be blessed through him. Part of Israel's job description as the people of God was to proclaim God's love to the nations. In Isaiah 42:6 and 49:6, the Lord calls them to be 'a light for the Gentiles', 'that you may bring my salvation to the ends of the earth.'

6. We also learn from the Old Testament that there will be a time of unprecedented 'tribulation' for God's people in the End times

Jeremiah is the prophet who introduces this theme of future tribulation. Again, Daniel sees tribulation for the saints before the end, in 7:21–25.

7. We also learn, from Old Testament prophecy, about the restoration of Jerusalem and Israel —both land and people

See especially Isaiah 2:2–4; Jeremiah 31; and Micah 4:1–5, to name only three references. But perhaps the most significant prophecy comes in Zechariah 9. Again, in verses 9ff., we see the wonderful concertina effect in biblical prophecy. You probably know verse 9 well because it regularly features on Palm Sunday —the prophecy of Christ entering Jerusalem, riding on a donkey. Then in verse 10 comes the proclamation of peace to the nations —that is the proclamation of the gospel among the nations by the followers of Christ; and then there is the millennial rule, the ultimate rule of Christ: 'His rule will extend from sea to sea... to the ends of the earth.' There is even a reference in verse 11 to the blood of the covenant.

In Zechariah 12:3, we read about a battle involving Jerusalem and the nations of the world; and then, in verse 10, Zechariah prophesies a 'spirit of grace and supplication' being poured out upon the people of Israel. Please note that they are not saved by any other means than we are. They, too, have to bow the knee to Christ; they have to accept him as Messiah, Saviour and Lord, but it is God's work. 'I will pour out on the house of David... a spirit of grace and supplication.' This is the grace that softens those hard hearts that rejected their Messiah; the spirit of supplication gives them the ability to call out for mercy and salvation. 'They will look on me, the one they have pierced, and they will mourn for him as one mourns for an only child, and grieve bitterly for him....' It is a wonderful promise for God's Old Testament people who, for centuries, have refused their Messiah and turned their backs on him, that the day will come when they will turn in great numbers to their Lord and their Saviour.

Just keep in mind that this was written some five hundred years before Jesus was born. In chapter 13, Zechariah speaks of the cleansing of the Jewish nation, and the ending of false religion. (See vv. 1f.) In chapter 14, we see a final battle again involving Jerusalem, and the Lord himself standing on the

Mount of Olives. (v. 4.) In Luke's account of the Ascension in 24:50, he tells us that it happened in the vicinity of Bethany; and Mark 11:1 tells us that Bethany was on the Mount of Olives; and Acts 1:11 records the angel asking the disciples, '...why do you stand here looking into the sky? This same Jesus, who has been taken from you into heaven, will come back in the same way you have seen him go into heaven' — meaning this same bodily Jesus they knew. And we have Zechariah saying (in 14:4) that the Lord will stand on the Mount of Olives. In 14:5, Zechariah sees the Lord coming with all his holy ones. Remember again the promise of Jesus (Matthew 24:30–31), 'They will see the Son of Man coming on the clouds of the sky, with power and great glory. And he will send his angels....' In Zechariah 14:8 we see living water flowing from Jerusalem (cp. Revelation 22:1); and in 14:9, we are told that, 'The LORD will be king over the whole earth.' In v. 16, Zechariah prophesies an annual celebration by the nations of the earth —the Feast of Tabernacles. The Feast of Tabernacles is the only Jewish feast to which Gentiles are invited. And we will see the significance that Jesus attaches to that feast.

The two prophetic books Ezekiel and Daniel contain so much material which foreshadows events picked up and developed by John in the Book of Revelation, that it is worth considering them in more detail. Ezekiel is one of the most esoteric, pictorial and wonderful books of the Old Testament. In the very first chapter, we find four living creatures bearing remarkable similarity to the four living creatures whom John sees in Revelation chapter 4. There is a reference to the battle of Gog and Magog, which again John depicts, in Revelation chapter 20. The closing nine chapters of Ezekiel describe a vision of the perfect temple, most probably a vision of the new Jerusalem. Notice the similarities. In Ezekiel chapter 47 we read that living water will come out of the city; and John writes (in Revelation 22) that the water of life will flow from the new Jerusalem. In Ezekiel's vision the water of life brings healing; it turns the Dead Sea into fresh water. In Revelation chapter 22 the water brings life, and the trees that grow by the river have leaves to heal the nations. In Ezekiel 48:30–35, the gates of the city match those of the new Jerusalem as described in Revelation chapter 21. So many jokes and cartoons feature the pearly gates, normally combining a bit of nimbus cumulus and some rather nice English Victorian stonework. But the pearly gates are real. They are in fact the gates of the new Jerusalem. Those are the gates through which Christ will lead the redeemed at the End. And it is wonderful that the name of the city Ezekiel sees, centuries before John, that once was *Jeru Salem* – the city of peace – is now to be *Jahweh Shama*, the Lord is here. In Revelation 21:3, a voice from the throne is heard, "Now the dwelling of God is with men, and he will live with them...." Emmanuel, the Lord, is with us.

Daniel is the fourth of the major prophets, and although people steer away from Daniel for much the same reasons as they do from the Book of Revelation, it is actually one of the easiest books to follow, because the interpretations are given within the text. We are going to be looking at Daniel in more detail when we study some of the texts of Revelation, but I just want to pick out a few things here. I am writing from the orthodox position, which the church has traditionally held, that Daniel was written in the sixth century before Jesus lived. Many scholars today do not accept that, mainly because they cannot believe that Daniel could be shown what was going to happen in the future.

In Daniel 7:13, Daniel sees 'one like a son of man, coming with the clouds of heaven.' Throughout the Gospels, Jesus deliberately called himself the Son of Man, knowing full well that the Jewish listeners would know exactly the significance of that title. And not only did he just call himself the Son of Man and accept the title, but he also spelt it out specifically in Matthew 24:30, when he said to his disciples, "They will see the Son of Man coming on the clouds of the sky, with power and great glory" —exactly the vision that Daniel saw. I find it both astonishing and wonderful that Daniel, all those centuries before Jesus was born, saw him as the Judge of all peoples coming to earth in the time of the End. In Daniel chapter 9, we find references to Christ's atoning death ('...the Anointed One will be cut off', v. 26); the activities of the End time beast, and the desolation in the temple. In chapter 12, Daniel foresees the resurrection: 'Multitudes who sleep in the dust of the earth will awake: some to everlasting life, others to shame and everlasting contempt' (v. 2). In Revelation chapter 20, John sees exactly the same thing: the dead brought to life, standing upon the earth in front of their Creator.

When it comes to the theology of the End times, the Old Testament is consistent in holding forth the promise of a renewed created order, from which sin and everything which mars life will be purged, and in which God will rule in righteousness and truth. So ask yourself, what are you looking forward to, today? Is it in line with God's word? The Book of Revelation, which is wholly consistent with the rest of God's full and final self-revelation in the whole of the Scriptures, shows us the truth about many things, which God wants his people to know; and he has been unveiling that truth through the ages.

Heavenly Father, I praise you for this great gift of your word. Lord, how clearly the Old Testament directs us to what shall be. Lord, help me to feed on your sacred Scriptures, to acknowledge them as your inspired gift to us, your very word of life. Father, may I be so transformed by your unveiling of the future that I shall never be the same again. Lord, let me have a yearning in my heart for the day when you return to this earth. As we are encouraged to do by Peter, let me speed the day of your coming, by living a godly and holy life. Come, Lord Jesus. Amen.

4

WHAT DOES JESUS SAY ABOUT THE END TIMES?

It is vital for us to look carefully at the teaching of Jesus himself on the End times, for a number of reasons:

Jesus 'opens up' and fulfils the Old Testament
Having witnessed the consistent voice of the Old Testament, I now want to consider the teaching of Jesus, the one to whom the Old Testament points, and the one in whom all its promises either have been, or will be, fulfilled. It is as though we see, in the Old Testament, a flower that is closed up; Jesus opens the flower, that we may see more clearly the things which are revealed there.

Jesus is the fulcrum of history, the fixed point about which human history revolves
Some people have described the Incarnation as being that narrow point in an egg timer, through which and from which all sand of time flows. Jesus is the lens by which we view everything. He, himself, ushers in the last days. Do you remember when Peter stands up on the day of Pentecost, the crowd gathers at the sound of the wind and the tongues, and Peter quotes from Joel 2:28, "In the last days, God says, I

will pour out my Spirit on all people" (Acts 2:17)? Peter has seen that prophecy fulfilled. The coming of Christ, the death of Christ, the resurrection of Christ and the outpouring of the Spirit, which is the gift of the risen and ascended Christ, mark the beginning of the 'last days'. And the 'last days' is Bible-speak for that period between Christ's first coming and his return. So we are living now in the last days, however long they last. This is the last hour, and there is a sense in which the prophetic clock stops ticking with Jesus. You may remember that when Jesus, in Luke 4:18ff., quoted Isaiah 61, "The Spirit of the Lord is on me...", he stops that reading half way through the verse. He ends with, "...to proclaim the year of the Lord's favour", and he omits 'and the day of vengeance of our God' (see Isaiah 61:2). In other words, the prophetic clock will begin ticking again when the signs, which we will look at in this chapter, begin to roll into play again.

All the promises of the Old Testament are reinterpreted in and through Jesus Christ

When you read the life of Jesus in the Gospels, it is remarkable how Jesus treads out the path of Israel all over again. There is the **flight into Egypt** of Joseph and Mary and the baby Jesus, recalling the flight of Joseph and his brothers into Egypt. There is then the **return from Egypt** and, as the people of Israel went through the Red Sea, so Christ goes to Jordan and is baptised. And just as all those of Israel who followed Moses stepping into the Red Sea, after him, were saved, so all those who, in faith and in baptism, place themselves in Christ, are saved. In St Paul's song of Christ's humility in Philippians 2, the apostle writes of Jesus, 'Who being in very nature God, did not consider equality with God something to be grasped, but made himself nothing, taking the very nature of a servant'. There are many other references in the New Testament to Christ lowering himself. It happens to be the case, incidentally, that the place where Jesus was baptised is in fact one of the lowest places on the surface of the earth. Immediately following Jesus' baptism he is driven **into the wilderness**, just as, immediately following the Red

Sea crossing, Israel began its own wilderness experience. The people of Israel wandered the wilderness for forty years, Christ for forty days —Christ treading out, as it were, the history of Israel. One of the high points of the journey of the Israelites with Moses was the visit to Mount Sinai and the giving of the law. Jesus, after his baptism, and after his wilderness experience, **climbs the Mount** and gives the sermon which is a re-stating of the law – 'Blessed are....' Jesus 'becomes' Israel in a typological sense. He becomes the **second Adam**, the new man, the one who, under obedience to the Father, is going to live life as life should be lived.

Let us consider briefly the way that Christ re-defines Israel. Paul taught the Roman Christians not to write off or neglect to pray for the Jewish people. He is absolutely clear that God has by no means finished with his chosen people. He is absolutely clear that it is the Jewish people to whom God has revealed his will and his grace. Jesus was the Jewish Messiah sent to the Jewish nation. Yet this truth is also like a flower which opens for us through the writing of Paul. For Paul sees in Christ the fulfilment of God's call upon Israel to '...bring my salvation to the ends of the earth' (Isaiah 49:6b). So, through the lens of his understanding of Christ, Paul re-defines what it means to be Jewish. In Romans 2:28 he shows how Jewishness is an inner reality. Jews are known for the physical, external mark of circumcision. Paul, himself a Jew, writes to the Galatians that, '...in Christ Jesus neither circumcision nor uncircumcision has any value. The only thing that counts is faith expressing itself through love.' In Romans 11, Paul teaches that 'all Israel will be saved' (v. 26), and goes on to affirm that this is because 'God's gifts and his call are irrevocable' (v. 29). Yet he also claims that it is possible, because of Jesus, for Gentiles to share in those gifts and that call. From verse 11 of chapter 11, and adopting a gardening analogy, he teaches that the Roman Gentile believers are like wild olive cuttings which have been grafted in to a cultivated olive tree (Israel). This argument finds its clearest expression in Ephesians 2:11–22. Paul begins by explaining that Gentiles were at one time 'separate from Christ, excluded from citizenship in Israel and foreigners to the covenants of the promise, without hope and without God in the world.' There is no doubt here then that the Jews are the chosen people of God, the ones to whom God has made promises and given hope. Then comes one of the great 'buts' of Scripture. 'But now in Christ Jesus you who once were far away have been brought near through the blood of Christ.' Paul goes on to explain that Jesus has 'destroyed the barrier' which kept Gentiles out 'by abolishing in his flesh the law with its commandments and regulations.' Why? 'His purpose was to create in himself one new man out of the two, thus making peace....' The result of Christ's sacrifice of himself on the cross, for the Gentiles, is then spelt out: 'Consequently, you are no longer foreigners and aliens, but fellow-citizens with God's people and members of God's household....' Praise God for his grace to us Gentiles!

When we think of the work Jesus has done in and through his death, for both Jew and Gentile, it is important that we remember that there are not two routes to peace with God: one ethnic, national, Zionistic route for the Jews as a nation, and, alternatively, that of faith in Jesus for Gentiles. Every human being who would be saved, Jew and Gentile alike, must come to God through Jesus Christ, the way, the truth and the life. Jesus was adamant that no one comes to the Father other than through himself. (See John 14:6.)

Famous last words

I have seen it many times. When someone knows they are near death, they often want to gather family and significant friends around them, and say some important things: an affirmation of love, or a final request, an apology perhaps, or clarification of a notion incorrectly held. Whatever it may be, you know it is going to be important because the person is near the end of their time on earth. The same was true of Jesus. Matthew, Mark and Luke all record in depth the teaching Jesus gave in the last few days of his earthly life, before he entered Jerusalem for the last time. Theologians call this teaching the Olivet discourse (referring as it does to the conversation Jesus had sitting with his disciples on the Mount of Olives), and you will find it in Matthew 24 and 25, Mark 13 and Luke 21. In the chart below I have attempted to show that all John's revelations fold into the pattern which Jesus sets on the Mount of Olives.

THE BOOK OF REVELATION AND THE OLIVET DISCOURSE

MATTHEW 24:1–3

The temple's future questioned

REVELATION 1, 4 & 5

The throne room of God revealed.

MATTHEW 24:4–29

Tribulation on earth

Concurrent signs (4–8)
War, rumours of war, famine

Two preliminary signs (9–14)
Persecution & Proclamation

First penultimate sign (15–26)
Desecration & Deceit

Second penultimate sign (29)
Convulsions in the heavens

REVELATION 6–18

Tribulation on earth

A repeating cycle of
War, rumours of war, famine

Persecution & Proclamation

Desecration & Deceit

Convulsions in the heavens

MATTHEW 24:30–31

The Son of Man
[The Passing of heaven and earth, v. 35]

REVELATION 19–22

The rider on the white horse
A new heaven and a new earth

MATTHEW 24:32–25:46

Warnings to be ready and to endure

REVELATION 2 & 3

Encouragements to be faithful and to overcome

We will now look at that pattern in more detail. At first sight, Jesus seems to say two contradictory things. On the one hand (in Matthew 24:36, 44), he teaches that you cannot and must not predict the time, even saying, "...the Son of Man will come at an hour when you do not expect him." But on the other hand (in verses 32 to 35) he teaches that you can and must read the signs; it is important to learn the lesson of the fig tree. Jesus is not in fact contradicting himself, the point is that we must avoid two dangerous extremes. On the one hand, we must not fall into the trap of trying to predict precisely when Jesus is going to return. So many Christians have done this, and I am sorry to say that Luther and Wesley were among them, although at least they were sensible enough to predict dates long after they would be dead! Jesus warns us not to do it. On the other hand, we ought not to be caught unaware when Christ does return.

We shall see a similar approach to the 'rapture of the saints' from Paul in his two letters to the church in Thessalonica. He teaches both that Christ will return quite unexpectedly, like a thief in the night, and yet also that Christians should not be taken by surprise. The obvious implication is that the householder who is aware that a thief is coming will take all precautions not to allow the thief access. The householder may not know precisely when the thief will strike, but need not be unprepared. A similar theme pervades Matthew 25, with its parables about the virtue of preparedness. So the life of the Christian is to be one of continual preparation and readiness. How we live now is crucial to whether we are going to be ready when Jesus returns. Using Matthew 24 – 25 as a basic text, we will now see the pattern that unfolds.

The request for a sign (Matthew 24:1–3)
Here we are given the reason for Jesus' 'eschatological' sermon. It is Tuesday of what we now call Holy Week, three days before Jesus will hang on a cross. Ever since he entered Jerusalem (in chapter 21), Jesus has been engaged in a constant running battle with his enemies in the Jewish religious hierarchy. He has driven the money changers from

the temple courts; healed the sick; cursed a fig tree; and been set a trap with one of Caesar's coins. He has spoken in parables about God's judgment coming upon Israel for rejecting him, and about God's grace in bringing in the Gentiles; he has answered the Sadducees' trick question about heaven; and pronounced a series of seven woes upon the scribes, Pharisees and teachers of the law.

Jesus is now alone, walking away from the temple precincts. Then his disciples catch up with him and draw his attention to the awesome beauty of the temple. Ah well, they were never great ones for sensitivity. Jesus himself gazes upon the temple and tells them that it will soon be utterly destroyed, with no stone left standing on another. Indeed, in AD 70 the Roman general who led his troops into Jerusalem gave the order that no stone was to be left standing one on another. No doubt there is enormous sadness in Jesus' voice, for Luke tells us of the Lord's great love for this city and its people: 'As he approached Jerusalem and saw the city, he wept over it' (19:41).

Then Jesus and the disciples walk to the Mount of Olives and sit together, gazing over the Temple Mount. The disciples have been shaken by Jesus' prophecy, and they ask two questions: when will the destruction of the temple happen and what will be the sign of his coming and of the end of the age? In his reply, Jesus displays one of the characteristics of prophecy which we noted earlier —the concertina effect. He swiftly moves from teaching about the temple to teaching about the very end of the age, and he uses the imminent destruction of the temple as a type, foreshadowing the end of the world, as we will see. This is how it all starts in Matthew 24:1–3. Jesus begins to talk about signs.

The concurrent signs: wars, rumours of war, natural disasters (Matthew 24:4–8)

Here we have a warning not to be deceived. It is absolutely vital that you are on your guard against deception. There are going to be so many attempts to deceive you. There have been many false christs and there will be many false christs in the future. Both Paul, in 2 Thessalonians 2, and John in his second letter, warn against deception, false prophets, and deceivers. Jesus warns of future wars, rumours of wars, civil wars, revolutions, famines and earthquakes. Well, we look around the world and we see it all happening. But Jesus tells us not to be alarmed! It is difficult not to be when we watch the news or read the papers. Fear is very real for the people of the world today, and with good reason. But Jesus tells us to be calm. The point of these concurrent signs is that they are happening all the time. They have happened in every generation, and they will happen right up until the End. (See Daniel 9:26). These are not signs that the End is imminent. So many Christians have been confused when they see major conflict. It happened during both World Wars. It is the same with natural disasters. They are happening all the time, and Jesus says that all of these things are only 'the beginning of birth pains'. I have witnessed my wife in the pain of childbirth on four occasions, and, although I cannot claim to know exactly how it feels, I can affirm that it is —well, painful. But, in fact, what a wonderful thing birth is! How quickly a mother forgets the pain in the sheer joy of holding new life in her arms. Birth pains are essentially positive. And Jesus says the convulsions that are going to come upon the earth will be like birth pains. Yes, times of great suffering and hardship, trial and tribulation lie ahead, but it is going to be worth it! St Paul takes up the theme in Romans 8:18ff. —'I consider that our present sufferings are not worth comparing with the glory that will be revealed in us ... the whole creation has been groaning as in the pains of childbirth right up to the present time.' In case we need more emphasis, let us remind ourselves of Jesus' words, "... the end will not come right away" (Luke 21:9b).

So the disciples (and we) are not to be fooled into hiding away or making all sorts of apocalyptic predictions, just because of wars and rumours of wars. They will always be around. There are other signs to come.

The two preliminary signs: worldwide persecution of the gospel community and worldwide proclamation of the gospel itself (Matthew 24:9–14)

The Book of Revelation teaches us that there is such a time as might be termed 'Satan's little season'. This has been variously referred to as the great apostasy, the great tribulation, the reign of the antichrist —all phrases which refer to that very short period which is going to come just before our world ends. There is, of course, a sense in which these two signs have been present throughout the Christian centuries. Christians have been persecuted, and the gospel has been proclaimed, in almost every part of the world. But there is also a clear indication (as we shall see in the Book of Revelation) that both will become far more intense in the very last years of human history on earth.

It is a sobering thought that persecution and hatred will become the norm for the Christian community. At this point in their narratives, Mark and Luke recall Jesus' promise that the Holy Spirit will aid Christians when they are called to give account for their faith.

More sobering is the prediction of Jesus that, "many will turn away from the faith and will betray and hate each other" (v. 10). In other words, in the last days of earth history, when the heat is turned up under the Christian community, there will be a significant apostasy. We know from history that there have always been those who have turned away from the faith rather than suffer —and it is not our place to condemn them from a position of comfort. But Jesus has warned us, so let us pray for grace and strength to stand firm if the time of testing should come during our lives. Given this teaching from Jesus, I think we have to ask ourselves what we mean as a church today when we talk about revival coming. There are many books on revival in our world today; many people in the church believe revival is coming. But the New Testament does not give us warrant for any sense of triumphalism, nor for the hope that the church is suddenly going to emerge as world ruler. Persecution and hatred will increasingly be the norm as we approach the End. Many will turn away from the faith and betray it, and hate one another. Paul writes to Timothy, '...in later times some will abandon the faith...' (1 Timothy 4:1). False prophets will appear. Many will be deceived. An increase in wickedness will lead to widespread apostasy. Look at 2 Timothy 3:12–14; 2 John 7, 8; Jude 18, 19, to see confirmation elsewhere in the New Testament.

The first penultimate sign — distress; the abomination of desolation; the tribulation (Matthew 24:15–26)

Again Jesus is talking both about the destruction of Jerusalem and also about the End time. The 'abomination that causes desolation' is a quotation from Daniel, the holy place a reference to the inner heart of the Jerusalem temple, the holy of holies, into which only the high priest was allowed and only on one day in the year. Luke adds that Jerusalem will be trampled 'until the times of the Gentiles are fulfilled'. But it is clear that Jesus is not just talking about the fall of Jerusalem, or he would have failed to answer the disciples' second question. Also he so stresses this time of tribulation, and that it immediately precedes the end of the world, that he is clearly talking about the End, although using what was shortly to happen in Jerusalem and to its inhabitants as a picture of what is to come.

The tribulation of the End will be so severe that there will have been nothing like it before: 'The distress of those days will be like nothing before and nothing since.' That was exactly what Daniel foresaw as well. In 2 Timothy 3, Paul writes of '...terrible times in the last days' (v. 1). The reason is the apostasy mentioned earlier, as many reject the Christian faith; Jesus says that those who reject the Christian faith will persecute those who remain firm. They are led by the antichrist. But, praise the Lord, the days will be cut short. (We will be looking at this peculiar little phrase from Daniel 7:25 – 'a time, times and half a time' – when we get to the relevant point in the Book of Revelation.)

In 2 Thessalonians 2, Paul talks of the 'man of lawlessness', who, 'will oppose and will exalt himself over everything that is called God or is worshipped, so that he sets himself up

60

in God's temple, proclaiming himself to be God' (v. 4). We are aware that there have been such characters throughout history, but Paul is specifically talking of the ultimate, End time antichrist. Note that, in the Greek, 'anti' means not 'against', but 'in place of', so we can expect, at least when the antichrist initially appears, that he will seem like a good thing. The antichrist will be very convincing; there will lots of 'miracles', lots of signs. But they will all be counterfeit. The antichrist may well bring a form of world peace, even a world government —who knows? If that seems far-fetched, a world economy would have seemed fanciful thinking just a generation ago, but it is virtually here as I write. But, however wonderful the antichrist seems, he will in fact be standing in place of Christ and, sooner or later, he will begin to expect worship and adulation —and then his real nature will be revealed. 'See', says Jesus, 'I have told you ahead of time.'

Do not listen to anybody who says the Son is here, the Christ has returned, the Messiah has come back. The coming of the Son of Man will be universally evident. It will be like lightning.

We should not be confused. Many have claimed to be messiahs, but the coming of the Son of Man will be absolutely evident, so you will not need anybody to tell you when he comes again. Wherever you are on the face of the planet, you will see him, if you are alive in those days.

The second penultimate sign —convulsions in the heavens (Matthew 24:29)

We have already read about that in the Old Testament. We will read a lot more about it in Revelation. In Matthew 24:29, Jesus teaches that this sign follows on immediately from the great distress. We cannot be particular or precise about exactly what is going to happen. When we read of darkness in the skies, turmoil among the stars and the shaking of heavenly bodies, it is clear that Jesus and John have something extraordinary in mind. Nations will be in perplexity. People will faint with terror.

But Christians should not be shaken. Think of a visit to

the theatre: you are in your seats, you have settled who is having which armrest, you have your popcorn, you are trying to keep the kids quiet, you are whispering away... and then the lights go out. Darkness is always the signal for the drama to begin. You are waiting for the curtain to open, for light to appear, and for the characters who are going to occupy the stage to be seen. And that is what will happen, though it will not merely be a dramatic presentation, it will be the real thing. Darkness will symbolise the beginning of the end, and then God himself will draw back the curtain separating time and eternity, earth and heaven, and light will spring forth revealing the main character, centre stage. The first words God is ever recorded as speaking are 'Let there be light.' Darkness has always been a symbol of chaos, disorder, and evil. John's Gospel opens with a description of Jesus as the light of the world: 'The light shines in the darkness, but the darkness has not understood [or overcome] it.' Later in his Gospel, John delivers his verdict: 'Light has come into the world, but men loved darkness instead of light because their deeds were evil. Everyone who does evil hates the light, and will not come into the light for fear that his deeds will be exposed' (3:19).

At the End, literal darkness will symbolise the world's darkest hour, when wickedness has reached its height, when the tribulation of the church is in full swing, and when believers can only wait with patient endurance, hanging on for light to be revealed.

The sign itself —the coming of the Son of Man
(Matthew 24:30–35)

Please do note – this is so, so important – that in the New Testament there is no understanding of the return of the Son of Man except in terms of a single event. Again, from America – and it is all wrapped up in dispensationalism and the rapture theories, which we will be looking at in detail later – you will hear about this coming and that coming; a secret coming, and then a public coming and then a third coming.... It is not in the New Testament. Be warned, and be aware of what the Scriptures teach. It is always a single event. "The sign of the Son of Man will appear". [Remember those wonderful words from Daniel 7:13, '...coming with the clouds of heaven.'] People have spent ages, rather emptily in many ways, thinking what the sign might be. In Mark we read, "At that time men will see the Son of Man coming in clouds with great power and glory" (13:26). I think that will do for me! All the nations of the earth will mourn. It does not say they will repent. We will see in Revelation the response of the kingdoms of earth to Christ's return. It is actually war, not repentance. But they will all mourn. The sound of the trumpet, the ram's horn or *shofar*, was what the Israelites used as a sign for the tribes to gather together. Perhaps something very like that sound will be heard. And the angels will be sent to gather the elect. Isn't that glorious! Wherever you are, if you are alive when this happens – you may not be, none of us may be – you will be gathered into the air. We will hear more about this later. Those who have preceded us in faith, who have died in Christ's peace, will be brought to life again. We will all meet the Lord in the air. (See 1 Thessalonians 4). Paul writes (in 1 Corinthians 15:51b) that we will be changed in the twinkling of an eye. The word 'rapture' has taken on connotations of joy, which it did not originally have, but which are very appropriate. And then there will be the judgment, as we see in Matthew 25, the separation of the righteous and the wicked.

I have listed in Appendix 2 other New Testament verses referring to the End times, and as you look through them, you will notice the same themes of which we read in the Old Testament —the coming judgment, the replacement (or renewal or re-creation) of the created order, the promise of a new created existence.

Consider especially 1 Thessalonians 4:13–5:11. It seems that Paul has received an enquiry from the church in Thessalonica about what will happen to those Christians who have already died by the time Christ returns in glory. Paul begins by writing, 'Brothers, we do not want you to be ignorant about those who fall asleep, or to grieve like the rest of men, who have no hope. We believe that Jesus died and rose again; and so we believe that God will bring with Jesus those who have fallen asleep in him.' In other words, all those who have died in the faith of Christ will accompany Jesus on his return. In verse 15, Paul then affirms, 'According to the Lord's own word', [here we refer back to the passage we were looking at, Matthew 24], 'we...who are left till the coming of the Lord, will certainly not precede those who have fallen asleep.' It helps here to remember Paul's statement in 1 Corinthians 15:52 that all this will happen in the twinkling of an eye. Those who have died and those who are still alive at the moment of Christ's return, will meet in an instant —in the air. It is a mind-blowing thought, especially in our modern, rational age. But it is the firm testimony of Scripture. Then comes 1 Thessalonians 4:16, the noisiest verse in the Bible: 'For the Lord himself will come down from heaven, with a loud command, with the voice of the archangel and with the trumpet call of God' —and then, 'the dead in Christ will rise first. After that, we who are still alive and are left will be caught up together with them in the clouds to meet the Lord in the air. And so we will be with the Lord forever. Therefore encourage each other with these words.'

The lesson of the fig tree: learning to read the signs
(Matthew 24:33–35)
Jesus goes on to encourage his disciples to learn to read the signs: "Now learn this lesson from the fig tree: As soon as its twigs get tender and its leaves come out, you know that summer is near. Even so, when you see all these things, you know that it [or 'he'] is near, right at the door. I tell you the truth, this generation [or 'this race' – the Greek can mean either] will certainly not pass away until all these things have happened."

Well, what on earth does 'near' mean? How soon is soon? Some verses from other parts of Scripture will help you to grasp God's understanding of time. 'The Lord's coming is near. The Judge is standing at the door' (James 5:8f); and, 'The end of all things is near' (1 Peter 4:7). Peter reveals that even in his own days, the non-return of Christ was leading 'scoffers' to ask "Where is this 'coming' he promised?" (See 2 Peter 3:3–18.) Peter goes on to explain that the day is coming, but yet a day is like a thousand years to God (quoting from Psalm 90), so the delay in Christ's return is due to his patience and mercy, not wanting anyone to perish, but as many as possible to come to faith. It is good news that the delay has been put into effect. If it were not for the delay, you and I would not have come into the kingdom. John says 'this is the last hour'. (See 1 John 2:18–27.) The antichrist is coming. His type is already abroad in the world.

Jesus says, 'Heaven and earth will pass away', and we are reminded of those great verses concerning the 'new heaven' and 'new earth' in the Old Testament; and in Romans 8:22, 'the whole creation has been groaning as in the pains of childbirth right up to the present time'; and Hebrews 1:12b, '...like a garment they will be changed'; and 2 Peter 3:7, '...the present heavens and earth are reserved for fire, being kept for the day of judgment and destruction of ungodly men.'

So, learn to read the signs, and remember that Jesus has ushered in the last days.

Two warnings
(Matthew 24:36–41)
Jesus concludes by giving two warnings, which mean do not predict and do not get caught out. In other words, be ready!

Firstly, we are unwise if we attempt to predict when Jesus will return. Jesus says, "No one knows about that day or hour, not even the angels in heaven, nor the Son, but only the Father." How much more specific could Jesus be? When someone comes to you and says it is going to happen on this date, remember Jesus' words. It is going to be just like the days of Noah. Life is going to go on as usual. What characterised the days of Noah? —false security and materialism; people eating and drinking, doing this, that and the other. Not that there is anything wrong with eating and drinking but, if it becomes all that you are interested in, it will blind you to the realities of life. Think of Luke 12 and the parable of the rich fool – the farmer who had so much money that he decides to tear down all his barns and build bigger barns and stuff them so full of food, and be the richest man around. He plans to eat and drink and be merry. But he dies that night and God says to him, 'You fool, you fool'.

We are called to prepare ourselves to meet our Lord, but not as though it were some hazy event on a distant horizon. We are called to prepare ourselves to meet him at a moment's notice, given the reality that none of us knows the time of our own death, which may well precede his coming. Luke adds the image of a trap closing unexpectedly. (See 21:34). Matthew talks of two men or women working side by side. One is taken, the other left. Again it is a picture of the rapture, of sudden judgment, of the sharp division between the righteous and the ungodly. "Therefore, keep watch, because you do not know on what day your Lord will come." Matthew then goes on to develop the image of the Lord's return as coming like a thief in the night. Therefore, be ready.

So, are we going to be caught unaware, or are we going to be prepared? In the First Epistle to the Thessalonians and in Matthew, we are shown two types of response to the return of Jesus. There will be those for whom it is a complete shock, who have made no preparation whatsoever, for whom it will be like a thief in the night, catching them completely unaware. But Paul writes to the Thessalonians, '...you... are not in darkness so that this day should surprise you like a thief' (1 Thessalonians 5:4). In the days of Noah, the vast majority of people were completely taken by surprise. No doubt those living near Noah, looking over the garden fence and seeing his massive boat under construction, made a few ripe comments. But Noah, his sons and his whole family were not caught out. God does not want us to be caught out, and he has warned us. On the one hand, Jesus teaches us that we do not know when he is coming back, but on the other hand that we are to read the signs. Similarly, Paul indicates both that it is going to be like a thief coming in the night, but also that Christians should not be caught unawares.

Jesus' teaching on the Mount of Olives concludes in Matthew 25 with four little picture parables, each of which prompts a question we need to ask ourselves:

- Are you a faithful servant, or are you a wicked servant?
- Are you wise and ready or foolish and unready?
- Are you an active servant, doing God's work? Or are you a lazy servant?
- Are you a sheep, or are you a goat?

We might summarise this by asking: How ready are you to welcome the Lord back to this earth? It is a good question, isn't it? How ready are you to meet Jesus face to face? One day, you will meet him, and it could be any day. You could put this another way: Do you know the Shepherd? In John chapter ten, Jesus said, "I know my sheep and my sheep know me..." (v. 14); and, "My sheep listen to my voice..." (v. 27). Do you recognise his voice? Paul and the other writers of the New Testament take up this theme. Paul writes, in 1 Corinthians 9:27, of his own fear of disqualification, '... so that after I have preached to others, I myself will not be disqualified for the prize.' If Paul needed to take care in that way, should not we, too? He writes to the Romans, having talked about them being grafted into the Jewish faith, and about the Jews who disbelieve being cut out, 'For if God did not spare the natural branches, he will not spare you either' (11:21). Paul continues to urge his readers to 'continue' in God's kindness, 'Otherwise you also will be cut off.' The writer to the Hebrews also raises this warning, in 2:1; 6:4–8; 12:14–29. In 2:3, we are faced with this sobering question, '... how shall we escape if we ignore such a great salvation?'

We began by reminding ourselves that God never unveils the future, except with the intention of transforming our present. And it all boils down to this, as Luke concludes in his version of the Olivet discourse, 'Be always on the watch, and pray that you may be able to escape all that is about to happen, and that you may be able to stand before the Son of Man' (21:36). How are you standing today?

Father, as your Son taught us to do, we pray that what we have learnt from the beginning may remain within us, so that we may remain in you. We ask it in his name. Amen.

PART THREE

The Book of Revelation

5

BACKSTAGE IN THE CONTROL ROOM OF HISTORY
Revelation 1, 4 & 5

In this chapter, I want to consider the view John is given of heaven in chapters one, four and five of the Book of Revelation. As we begin the study of this part of the text of Revelation, we do well to bear in mind certain principles. First of all, there are many areas of interpretation of Revelation about which we cannot afford to be too dogmatic —certainly not to the point of losing fellowship with other Christians. This is always a danger. It is somewhat like the debate that has raged for centuries over infant baptism or adult baptism. You cannot really prove either case from the Bible or from history, and both sides really just end up talking endlessly to each other. So we do not want to be divided by our interpretations in such areas. Secondly, the point of biblical teaching is never merely to inform you. It is never merely to fill your head with knowledge. The real point of biblical teaching is not information, but transformation. Biblical teaching is to mould your heart and change your life. We must always be addressing to ourselves the questions: 'What must be different now because of what I have learnt?' 'What must change in the way that I live, because of what I have read or heard?'

I SAW HEAVEN OPENED

When I was working as a chaplain in one of the Cambridge colleges, I also worked as one of the university's photographers. One of my most fascinating jobs was taking pictures of the Vice Chancellor of the University, in the University Control Room. Hitherto, I had no idea of its existence. I had studied at Cambridge, walked the streets of Cambridge, visited all of the famous buildings, and now I was working for one of the colleges; but I had no idea there was a control room —and that is exactly what they call it. In this control room there are no windows, but there are banks upon banks of monitors, with views of the streets of central Cambridge, and of various university buildings, shown from different angles. From this room, the entire security of the university is controlled and directed. After that particular assignment I was forever aware of being watched wherever I went! And there is something of that ceaseless surveillance as we come to know and love God. The letters to the seven churches each begin with the Lord saying 'I know'. In our church we sometimes use a prayer which acknowledges that God is one 'unto whom all hearts are open, all desires known, and from whom no secrets are hidden'.

Think back to a trip to the theatre or cinema. You are very aware of the actors, the script that is being spoken, the scenery and the props. How easy it is simply to forget the significance of the director. Yet it is the director who is responsible for every word that is spoken, every gesture that is given, the different camera angles, and the way that the actors play their parts together. 'All the world's a stage...' said Shakespeare. Human life has a plot. Human history has a destination. And the Bible reveals something of that plot. This does not mean that we are puppets, pulled by hidden strings —far from it! Each of us has the choice as to what we will make of our 'character'. And yet the Bible tells us that God has designed a role for each of us, and it is the discovery of that role which gives our life meaning and purpose. It is the discovery of that role which prevents the feeling that we are mere accidents of cosmic chance.

Sadly, though, the human race has, for the most part, lost the script. We do not know our lines. We cannot see the plot. Many even doubt that the director exists at all. The Book of Revelation is perhaps the supreme expression of Scripture's insistence that the world has a director, who is moving according to his purposes, according to his timescale; that there is one who has written the script, and who has sealed the final acts of human history. In these opening chapters of his Revelation, John is, as it were, taken into the divine control room, the cosmic nerve centre —or, if you like, John is taken behind the scenes to see the director's chair, to see the script of the world's future.

In the very first verse of chapter one, John tells us the purpose for which these revelations were given to him by Jesus Christ: to 'show his servants what must soon take place.' The future is unveiled that we might be transformed. The author then introduces himself to us, as John, servant of Jesus Christ. His name appears again in verses 4 and 9 of this first chapter. Many people have tried to argue that this was a different John from the apostle John – the one who wrote the Gospel and the three letters – and the reason that they say that is because the writing of Revelation is so different from his other works. Well, I guess that if people living several hundred years from now went to the cinema and watched 'Raiders of the Lost Ark', 'ET', and then 'Schindler's List', they might easily conclude that they were the work of three different people, though they would be wrong.

The very fact that John only needs to use his name is an indication of who he is. We can be fairly sure that this is John, the apostle, Jesus' closest friend in his time on earth.

CHAPTER ONE — ONE LIKE A SON OF MAN

What a beautiful description John gives us, of God the Father and of Jesus Christ, from verse 4 onwards: '...him who is, and who was, and who is to come'; an echo of the divine name given by God to Moses in Exodus, 'I am who I am.' The author of Hebrews describes Jesus as 'the same yesterday and today and for ever.' (See Hebrews 13:8.)

We are introduced straightaway to the number seven, which will occur 52 times during the course of the book. Seven times the word 'blessed' is used; there are seven churches, seven spirits and so on. The lamb is mentioned 7 times 4 times – 28 occasions. Seven is a symbol of fullness, of completion.

See how John describes Jesus, in verse 5, as 'the faithful witness, the firstborn from the dead, and the ruler of the kings of the earth'. It is this Jesus '...who loves us and has freed us from our sins by his blood, and has made us to be a kingdom and priests to serve his God and Father.' The expression 'kingdom of priests' is used in the Old Testament, in Exodus 19:6, to describe the Old Testament people of God; and St Peter uses the word 'priesthood' in 1 Peter 2:5 and 9 to describe the New Testament people of God. That is what we are. I do not know how kingly or priestly you feel as you read this, but the Bible teaches that if you have placed your faith in Jesus Christ, then he has made you part of his royal priesthood. If we truly believed that, what would change about our lives today?

In verse 7, John introduces one of the remarkable features of the Book of Revelation —we in fact glimpse the end on several occasions throughout the book before we actually arrive at chapters 21 and 22.

'He is coming with the clouds'. This is what Daniel prophesied, what Zechariah 'saw' with his prophetic sight, and what Jesus told us will happen. Even those who pierced him will see. The nations of the earth will mourn. What a day it will be when we see the Lord coming on the clouds of glory. We cannot possibly imagine it. Maybe, like me, you

74

are praying that it might be in our day; that you and I might see. What a day it will be! We do not know when it will be, we do not make any foolish predictions; but we long for that day when we will see him coming.

Then the Lord himself speaks. "'I am the Alpha and the Omega", says the Lord God, who is, and who was, and who is to come' —and do notice that, again, everything that is said of God the Father in Revelation is also said of Jesus. In 1:17 Jesus says, "I am the beginning and the end, the first, the last, the Alpha, the Omega", the first and last letters of the Greek alphabet signalling one who holds everything together.

How would these words have been received by the members of those seven churches in what is now western Turkey —Ephesus, Smyrna, and the rest? Christians were already finding that holding the faith was hard. They faced a materialistic and consumer-driven society; they lived among people who were constantly waiting for the latest robes, the latest perfumes, the latest spices, the latest luxuries to come by trade. They faced a plethora of competing spiritualities, world views, philosophies, religions, faiths. They lived in a world where sexual decadence was just the tip of an iceberg of almost unrestrained moral corruption. And they faced pressure from the authorities to conform to the practice of emperor worship. This pressure was rapidly turning into persecution for Christians who refused to bow the knee to Caesar. Not too dissimilar to today, then; aren't we aware of a consumer-mad society, the competing world-views and spiritualities knocking on our doors daily, a society which is morally bankrupt? And oh yes, the pressure from the authorities —we may not acknowledge it, but it is there: Sunday trading now is the norm in the UK; some nine million people regularly work on Sunday, and many parents spend less and less time with their children; and there is pressure from the media upon our leaders to water down our moral stance as a church. The pressure is there all right. The pressure will grow worse. And maybe we, like John's first readers, are tempted to say 'Where is God? Why does evil seem so rampant? Why do the forces of darkness seem so triumphant? Where is the vindication promised by God? Where is history going? Is it going anywhere? Is God ever going to act?' Do you ever feel like that when you watch the news and you see carnage in so many different parts of the world? When is God going to act?

Note that John is right there with his readers, in 1:9, 'I John, your brother and companion in the suffering and kingdom and patient endurance that are ours in Jesus....' John knows only too well what they face. In fact they are missing his leadership and his presence at this precise moment because he is exiled on the Roman penal colony of Patmos, because of his refusal to compromise on his faith. And all this happens on the Lord's Day, which as we have already noted did not mean Sunday. This was the day when incense was to be burnt on the altars of all the temples, and the people were required to engage in a special liturgy of worship to the emperor. On that very day the revelation of God's sovereignty breaks in and a loud voice, like a trumpet, says, 'Write on a scroll what you see....'

John turns around, '...to see the voice that was speaking'. There follows a description of Jesus Christ in all his risen, ascended glory. It is important to note several things about the symbolism used by John as he gazes upon the Son of Man.

First of all, he is attempting not so much to describe geography or time or place, but rather the emotional impact of the experience he is having. We must not expect always to be able to explain and interpret every last little bit of this book. Think of it, if you will, rather as a gallery hung with impressionist paintings, rather than a photographic record presented to a coroner.

Secondly, John is drawing on a fund of apocalyptic imagery from the Old Testament: Daniel, Ezekiel, Zechariah, the apocryphal books of Ezra, and so on. It seems that John is deliberately interpreting his vision into apocalyptic conventions, so his readers would understand what he is saying. Of course, words written in code are never meant to be pronounced, but rather deciphered. And that is our work, as we study Revelation. So let us not be put off by the symbolism. John here sees someone like a Son of Man —and anyone with any remote understanding of Jewish history would be right back in Daniel 7. They would know that here was the Messiah, the promised one, the one beloved of the prophets, the one who is and will be king of all. He is wearing a robe that goes right down to his feet; and instantly their minds would have been drawn to the high priest's robe (Exodus 28 and 29). And yet, he is also described, in verse 14, as like the Ancient of Days in Daniel —'His head and hair were white like wool, as white as snow, and his eyes were like blazing fire'. If you go back to Daniel 7:9f., you will find that that is the description of God, the Father. John fuses the imagery of the Old Testament, in order to present the majesty of the risen Christ. We read in verse 16 that he has a double edged sword coming out of his mouth and we think of the sword of judgment in Isaiah 49, or in Hebrews, 'For the word of God is living and active. Sharper than any double-edged sword, it penetrates even to dividing soul and spirit...' (Hebrews 4:12a).

No wonder that John's response to this overwhelming vision is physical as well as emotional —he falls at Jesus' feet 'as though dead'. John has an experience which would have been entirely familiar to the prophets of old. There is something about the sheer majesty of the Lord that makes it hard to remain standing up. Here, we are told, as throughout Scripture, that a perfectly proper response to an encounter with God is to fall over. It has always baffled me that people falling down before the presence of the Lord is so maligned in some sections of the church. I can understand the press not liking it much, although it is rather amusing that they refer to the 'strange practice' of falling over. How much practice does falling over take? The biblical witness is that falling over in the presence of God is quite normal. One of my passions is the belief that what makes us quintessentially human is that, somewhere inside us, there is a desperate urge to know the truth. The Christian faith centres around a person who *is* the truth. When we encounter him, when we are met by the truth, when we are grasped by the truth, Jesus, the only proper response is to bow the knee before him in loving adoration and obedience. How often does our church worship lead us into that place where we can barely stand in God's presence?

Then, in the midst of this majestic vision of Christ, there is the human touch of Jesus, in verse 17, in response to John's collapse. Jesus places his right hand on John and says, 'Do not be afraid.' We are reminded of the mount of the transfiguration. Peter, James and John have gone up the mountain with Jesus, and they are overawed by the transformation that comes upon him, as he shines with a blinding glory, and Moses and Elijah appear beside him; they fall down, and it is at that point that Jesus comes and touches them — how beautifully human, how movingly compassionate, is our Lord.

"I am the First and the Last. I am...." —again we meet the Old Testament title for God. "I am the Living One; I was dead, and behold I am alive for ever and ever! And I hold the keys of death and Hades." Jesus has achieved total victory over death, which Paul tells us in 1 Corinthians 15 is the final enemy. Because of Jesus' death and resurrection, we need not fear it any more.

CHAPTERS 4 & 5
THE THRONE, THE SCROLL AND THE LAMB

Chapters 4 and 5 are taken up with three great symbols: the Lamb, the scroll and the throne. Or, using our theatrical analogy, the director's chair, the missing script and the leading man.

Let us just recap again, because it is important to remember the situation into which John writes: persecution, oppression, temptation, faith being severely tested, things not going well for the church. Is the church going to survive the first century of its existence? Jesus had proclaimed that, with his coming, the kingdom was drawing near, and his teaching indicated that the final act of earth history was beginning to unfold. Many were now dying, some as martyrs at the point of the sword. The teaching of Jesus suggested that the devil was no longer to be feared, but does experience in the world not tell us that the devil is taking centre stage? When the church is tested by persecution, temptation and oppression, the one thing it needs above all is a vision of God's sovereignty —and that is Revelation. John saw 'a door standing open in heaven' —what a glorious privilege, to look behind the scenes of history. "Come up here, and I will show you...." These words instantly correct some Christian views of the world as being so desperately evil that there is no longer any point trying. You may have met Christians who almost look forward with glee to the world's destruction because the world is so evil we had better get it over with as soon as possible; there is no point in evangelism, no point in social action, no point in ecological concerns – let's just get the fireball going, the quicker the better – because the devil has taken charge.

Against that, John has seen the 'control room' and the 'director's chair'. You will be aware as you read these words in Chapter 4, how John blends imagery from several Old Testament sources —chiefly two:

1. Isaiah 6 - that glorious vision which Isaiah receives in the temple. Good King Uzziah has just died, and Isaiah is probably wondering who is going to take the throne now. What sort of rascal are we going to have on the throne? And suddenly the temple erupts with a vision of God's glory which is so great that only a little bit of the hem of God's robe is visible.

2. Ezekiel 1. Like John, Ezekiel is a servant of God in exile, wandering in despair by the river, yet suddenly engulfed by a storm of God's glory. You will see the similarities: the thunder, the lightning, the rainbow emerald, the sea of glass, the sapphire, the jasper, the carnelian. The description of the four living creatures in John's vision is clearly taken from Ezekiel 1:10.

Additionally, thunder and lightning remind us of the giving of the law on Sinai.

Yet John also introduces elements that are unique to his own vision. His description of the seven spirits [or sevenfold Spirit] of God, speaks of the fullness of God's power.

John also sees twenty-four elders, each seated on a separate throne. Some argue that this is an order of angels, although 'elder' is normally used in the New Testament of a human. It is more likely, then, that this is a symbolic representation of the perfect people of God: the twelve patriarchs of Israel; the twelve apostles of the church. But do remember that we are not to be dogmatic here. If we start getting bogged down in our interpretation of who exactly the twenty-four elders are, we have lost the plot. John is not trying to teach us the geography of heaven, but to convey the wonder of a vision of a God who sits enthroned above all, ceaselessly adored by countless beings. We are not meant to argue detail so much as to be struck dumb with awe at the glory of the God we worship. In the song of heaven which is sung over and over again, 'Holy, holy, holy is the Lord God Almighty', God is acclaimed as the One who was and is and is to come, eternally unchanging. John makes it absolutely clear that God is directing, he is the one who holds the script; this is the God who knows how all things will be, no matter what events on the stage of history may appear to show.

For Christians – whether facing Roman persecution in the first century, or facing the seduction of pluralism in the twenty-first — this is not merely some academic point of pietistic devotion, but a powerful, political statement of enormous practical application. There are huge political implications of Christian worship. Look at 4:10 —what do the elders do as they worship? They lay their crowns before the throne. That was the act of obeisance, instituted by Alexander the Great and continued by the kings that followed him. And in verse 11, 'You are worthy' is lifted directly from the liturgy of the emperor worship of ancient Rome. It is what the people of the Roman Empire, including the Christians living under Rome, were expected to chant, especially on the Lord's Day: 'You are worthy.' John's vision is revealing the falsehood of all human power, the emptiness of human tyranny. Do not worship them, John teaches, for the future of the world does not lie in the hands of human rulers. The petty favours that they might be able to offer you – or even the harsh torture with which they might threaten you – are as nothing compared with what God has in store for those who love him. I can show you a loftier throne, a greater king.

The worship of heaven is a powerful assertion of human freedom in the face of tyranny. It is far more powerful than the assassin's bullet or bomb. Christians do not need to assassinate their tyrants, because they are not important enough. They may lock us up, they may cramp our style, they may take our lives; but they cannot have our worship, for we have seen heaven opened, we have seen the one sitting on the throne. Christian worship is an act of political will, as well as an act of devotion. When we worship – however imperfectly – here on earth, we join the chorus of heaven in declaring that nobody, and I mean nobody – be it democratically elected government or military regime – has the right to receive what is due to our God. Do you see how far-reaching our worship is? Do you see how Christian worship challenges the very foundations of human tyranny and all the regimes that take to themselves the attributes that properly belong to God? And that is why nearly every political tyranny that this world has ever known has sought to prevent God's people from worshipping.

But wait a moment. As we move into chapter five, there seems – even in the throne room – to be a problem. John sees, in the right hand of the one sitting on the throne, a scroll. But there is a question being asked over and over again; and it is a question that cannot be answered (verses 1–3). We need to understand what this scroll is. We are helped in this, because it appears twice in the Old Testament, in Ezekiel chapter 2 and Zechariah chapter 5 —a scroll with writing on both sides (quite specific), and Ezekiel tells us that the contents are lament, mourning and woe. In other words, the scroll that is held in the right hand of him who sits on the throne is a scroll of judgment. But we also encounter it later in Revelation when we read that it is the Book of Life, and that it belongs to the Lamb who was slain —bringing us right back here into chapter five. This is the scroll of judgment and of destiny, upon which is written the final details of our planet's existence. It contains the cast list, who will take their bow at the final curtain. We will see that in the next chapter, as the seals begin to be broken, because that is precisely what happens: woe, lament and mourning. This, then, is the missing script: God's plan to judge the world, to redeem his people, to consummate history, is all here. Yet the extraordinary thing is that it is secret, it is sealed; and nobody can be found to break the seals. No one can be found to open it, nor even risk a peep inside. What an astonishing thought that God's final purposes cannot be brought to be, that God's judgment cannot be executed. It is like a huge ocean liner held under wraps for want of somebody to cut the ribbon. The whole of human history's future hangs in the balance, whilst this question reverberates around heaven: Who is worthy? And John weeps. He weeps and he weeps and he weeps. John's tears symbolize the agony of the human condition, because all of us, deep down somewhere, know that our life is supposed to have purpose. We talk about progress precisely because this is what our spirits tell us —that we are going somewhere, that we are supposed to be improving. But the tragedy of the human condition is that we just cannot achieve it. Progress remains a tantalizing dream that haunts our sleep and yet remains just out of touch. John's tears, it seems to me, echo the agony of countless millions who feel the frustration and the despair of injustice and evil and depression. Cannot God do something? Cannot God act? Will God not intervene to wrap everything up? Can God's judgment be thwarted? Even the angels are asking the question; and until the question is answered the drama of human history remains locked away in the interval before the final act; and all we can do is weep and weep for paradise lost.

But the deadlock is broken when one of the elders tells John that the Lion of Judah, the Root of David – and all John's readers would know that these titles mean no one but the

Messiah – has triumphed. Finally, the question in heaven is answered. The one promised by the prophets – the Son of David, the Lion of Judah – is able to open the scroll.

Here is one of John's masterstrokes of symbolism, because when he looks for the lion, what does he see? In verse 6, 'a Lamb, looking as if it had been slain'. What a poignant moment. A lamb is weak, harmless, and innocent. It is supremely an animal of sacrifice. Yet this lamb has seven horns, symbolizing total power, seven eyes symbolizing all-encompassing knowledge – hardly Mary's little lamb, then. This glorious paradox of victory from suffering, a triumph from failure —the Lion of Judah is a lamb looking as if it were slain. Remember that right at the beginning of John's Gospel, when John the Baptist sees Jesus approaching him at the river Jordan, he calls out, "Behold the Lamb of God, who takes away the sin of the world!" It is easy to gloss over that acclamation, but I think John must have been ashen as he said those words. Rather than a shout of acclamation, I hear the awe of comprehension, as John realizes, perhaps for the first time, that his own cousin is to become God's ultimate sacrifice – that there will be no last-minute reprieve as there was for Isaac on Mount Moriah; that the world will find the possibility of the forgiveness of sins through the death of the carpenter from Nazareth.

These two chapters emphasize two themes which are central to the whole of the New Testament.

The pivotal significance of the cross

Note (in 5:9) that, because the Lamb is able to open the seals, heaven is given a new song. 'You are worthy to take the scroll.' Why? Not because the Lamb is the pre-existent Son of God, the agent of creation or anything like that, even though he is. No, you are worthy because you were slain. The Lamb is worthy because of the cross, because his blood redeemed people for God. And this helps to explain one of the deepest mysteries and puzzles of the human situation. On the one hand, we believe that God pre-determines history, that he knows the beginning from the end, as the prophet Isaiah puts it; and yet the Bible also insists that history is significant – that what you and I do, at any given point, is significant.

Have you actually felt, 'Well, if God knows what is going to happen, then why bother going through with this at all?' The final act is planned, the elect are chosen, the script is written; but the script is sealed and can only be unsealed by the events which occur within history. The God who pre-determines all things has made his own purposes entirely dependent upon one scene in human history. Everything that God purposed for the world, for redemption, for re-creation, literally hangs on the cross. If Jesus had said 'no', if Jesus had bottled out, the question 'Who is worthy?' would still be echoing round heaven today, and you and I would be eternally lost. It is the blood of Christ that redeems us. The director, you might say, is keeping everybody in suspense, until the leading man steps onto centre stage —the hero who alone is worthy. And so only in the aftermath of the cross can this question be answered. Only now can heaven sing a new song. The world may see the crucifixion of Christ in many different ways: the execution of a political revolutionary; the end of a very good life. But heaven sees the death of Christ as everything. The cross has changed human history, but it has also changed heaven; and now human history can finally move to its end.

The exalted position of Jesus

Where is the Lamb? In the centre of the throne. He shares the adoration of the heavenly hosts; the elders now cast their crowns before him, and sing to him the song that was sung for the Father. Nowhere in Scripture is there a more glorious scene than this. The Hallelujah Chorus was inspired by these words. Nowhere in the New Testament is there a clearer statement that Jesus is God. Our world has all sorts of views about who Jesus was; the only Jesus heaven knows is the supreme ruler of all, the Lamb of God, the king of the universe, the one who is enthroned forever, sitting in the majesty and glory and wonder of heaven. John ran out of words, and so do we. And yet it is this Jesus, gloriously king over the universe, who offers to be your friend and your companion upon the journey of life. We often say that, in this life, it is not what you know so much as who you know. Well, that is certainly true of the life to come. Do you know the Lamb of God? Do you know Jesus Christ as Saviour and Lord? The Book of Revelation will insist that even now the seals of earth's final act are being broken, that there can be no more thwarting God's finally acting in glorious judgment upon the world. To sum up with our theatrical metaphor, the leading man is assembling the entire cast for their final bow —and, as in all good theatre performances, those of us who take part in that final bow will be dressed in more glorious costumes than we have ever worn during the play. The writer to the Hebrews calls those who have joined Jesus in heaven 'the great company of witnesses' – don't you just long to be part of that? Don't you long to take centre stage with Jesus in the final moment of this present age? The invitation is there —it is offered to all who place their faith and trust in him. And unlike any dramatic performance, this is the real thing, not a work of fantasy or the imagination.

If you have not already given your life to Christ, asked him to be your Lord and Saviour, and received him, I urge you to do so now. Here is a prayer you could use:

Lord God, I acknowledge that my sins have separated me from you. I am sorry for them, I turn from them, and I ask your forgiveness. Thank you that you sent your Son Jesus Christ to die for me on the cross of Calvary, so that I may be forgiven. Jesus, thank you for dying for me, in my place; I receive you as my Saviour and Lord. I give you my life now and I ask you to come and dwell in me. Baptise me now in your Holy Spirit. I declare that I am born again; a child of yours, and saved by your grace. Keep me faithful to you all the days of my life. Amen.

If you prayed that prayer, tell someone you trust, at a church where the Bible is believed.

6

TROUBLES UPON EARTH

Revelation 6:1 – 8:5

Here is a brief outline of the structure of the Book of Revelation:

Chapters:

1–3	THE PRESENT —Earth *Things must be put right now.*
4–5	PRESENT —Heaven
6–18	FUTURE —Earth (with glimpses of heaven) *The bad news —things will get worse before they get better.*
19	THE RETURN OF CHRIST
20–22	FUTURE —Heaven on earth *The good news —things will get much better after they get worse.*

There are three problems to consider as we look at chapters 6–18:

1. The order of events
In what order did these visions happen? Do they proceed chronologically, one after the other?

2. The meaning of the symbols
The two witnesses of chapter 11; the woman and the child of chapter 12; the beasts of chapter 13. Who on earth are they?

3. The timing of fulfilment
For example, when we read in Revelation 12 that Satan is hurled to earth, what do we make of the reference of Jesus, after the return of the 72, to Satan falling like lightning from heaven? (See Luke 10:18). What is the meaning of the phrases that punctuate John's visions: 'After this', 'then I looked', 'then I heard' —does it actually mean that each successive vision will follow chronologically in earth history?

If I had to imagine a subtitle for the Book of Revelation, I would be tempted by this: 'A roller coaster ride set within a gallery hung with impressionist art'. You know the feeling you get from a roller coaster ride —I hate them! But maybe you enjoy that mixture of exhilaration and utter fear as you begin that slow climb upwards: you are locked in, you have checked about fifty times that the restraint is actually on, and you are getting higher and higher, a slow ascent, wonderful yet fearful. That is what we looked at in the last chapter as we considered Revelation 4 and 5 —the ascent upwards. And suddenly now we are plunging down, rushing ahead at an incredible speed, the future rushing towards us, rushing past us; and the ride offers us multiple glimpses of the same thing, just as a roller coaster ride when you see various points over and over again. You glimpse the end of the ride almost at the beginning, as we did in Revelation 1:7 —yet you do not actually come to it until you have seen it from different angles several times more. That, for me, is something of what the Book of Revelation is like. That is what it is going to be like for us as we work our way through it. Sometimes the end will seem near, sometimes it will seem far away. And these twists and turns and repeated views are expressed through three features, which are seemingly, although not actually, scattered randomly throughout the text —almost to interrupt the flow.

1. Digressions or insertions
Chapter 7, which we shall consider below, is an insertion between the breaking of the seals. In chapter 6 we see the first six seals broken and then we have to wait a whole chapter before the seventh is broken.

2. Recapitulations
The seventh seal, the seventh trumpet, the seventh bowl —all seem to be talking about the same thing. Earthquakes happen all the way through the book.

3. Anticipations
Armageddon is first mentioned in chapter 16 but not actually detailed until chapter 19; John first mentions Jesus riding to earth on the clouds in chapter 1, but we do not in fact see him until chapter 19; and the End itself is glimpsed throughout the book, at various corners of the roller coaster ride.

LOOKING FROM BOTH SIDES
Part of the reason for this roller coaster effect is that John's visions swing between earth and heaven, seeing the same scene or the same event from those two different perspectives. We see this classically in chapters 6 and 7, where John's vision seems to swing between pessimism and optimism. Human history has swung between the two. The beginning of the twentieth century in Britain, for example, saw the country basking in the glories of the Edwardian period, the 'golden age' of empire. Industrial 'progress' was promising a humanistic utopia, achieved by technological marvels and scientific breakthroughs. Today, the mood has changed to one of pessimism. Are we actually going to make it?

Chapters 6 and 7 achieve a biblical balance between

apparent 'pessimism' and 'optimism', mainly because the perspectives of earth and heaven are very different. It seems to me that Christians, in following John's visions, are called to realism. Remember what we have said all the way through: that the unveiling of the future only occurs in order to transform the now. We should not be naively optimistic about some future utopia, achieved by political advances or scientific breakthrough; but nor should we share the terror of the inhabitants of earth, on the day when the stars fall and the world begins to crack. "I have told you ahead of time", said Jesus in Matthew 24:25. Realism is always based on the facts; and, as Christians, we believe that the Book of Revelation gives us the facts on which to base our realism.

A comparison of the 7 seals (ch. 6), the 7 trumpets (chs. 8 & 9) and the 7 bowls (chs. 15–16)

THE SEALS (ch. 6)	THE TRUMPETS (chs. 8–9)	THE BOWLS (chs. 15–16)
1. A white horse	Earth	Earth
2. A red horse	Sea	Sea
3. A black horse	Rivers/springs	Rivers/springs
4. A pale horse	Sun	Sun
5. Souls of martyrs	The Abyss (locusts)	Throne of the Beast
6. Great earthquake (144,000 sealed) (great multitude)	Euphrates (mass death) (the angel/little scroll) (the two witnesses)	Euphrates (Armageddon)
7. Silence in heaven (earthquake)	Proclamation of God's kingdom (earthquake)	Proclamation — 'It is done' (earthquake)

THE SEVEN SEALS OF CHAPTER 6

Let us rejoin our text and plunge back into the story, into John's mind and spirit on that long ago day on Patmos, when the Lamb of God begins to break the seals upon the scroll of destiny. We meet straightaway a white horse, with a rider; and we know, because we know the story, that in fact there are going to be four horses. We may also know, if we know our Old Testament, that they are not original to John. We have met them before in Zechariah 6, when we are told that they are winds or spirits or angels sent out from God to patrol the earth. The title 'the four horsemen of the apocalypse' has really come to us lately through Dürer's painting of that title; and Billy Graham has written a book 'Approaching Hoofbeats' about these four horsemen. See opposite a chart comparing the seven seals, trumpets and bowls, which we will refer to from time to time in this and later chapters.

6:1–2
The first seal: a white horse —the spirit of imperialism
Now this first horseman has often been identified with Jesus. After all, in Revelation 19 we will meet another white horse, whose rider is unmistakably Christ —white, say the scholars, is the colour of heaven.

But I am not at all convinced that this first rider is Jesus. For a start, John makes him one among four. Is that really likely, given the vision of Jesus which John has received? To John's early readers, white would simply have been the colour of victory. When a Roman emperor or general returned to Rome after a successful military campaign, he always rode a white horse It simply means victory. All four horsemen are agents of disaster and doom. It seems to me that what we have here – the white horse – is the spirit of imperialism. Of course, in John's day, Rome would have been the current example, but John is such a brilliant writer (I hope you are beginning to realise how brilliant and subtle he is) because, even in this description, there is a hint that even mighty Rome will one day fall. Notice the weapon that the rider on the white horse is given —a bow. Now that is not a Roman weapon: the Romans did not use bows at all. This is a Parthian weapon: it is the curved bow of the hordes who, even in John's day, were beginning to attack the fringes of the empire and who, one day, of course, would carve out an empire of their own. It seems to me that what we have here, in this horse, is the spirit of all expansionist militarism: the Romans, the Parthians, the British, the Germans, the Russians, the Americans —the whole lot of them. The spirit of imperialism lives on; the white horse rides out today.

6:3–4
The second seal: a red horse —the spirit of revolution
This horse's rider 'was given power to take peace from the earth and to make men slay each other. To him was given a large sword.' At first reading it sounds as though this is the same horse as the first in a different colour. But again, John is more subtle, because one of the ironies of imperialism is that it brings peace. Think of the upsurge in violence in some of the former Soviet republics, which would have been unthinkable under Soviet rule. I am not saying that Soviet rule was good, but it brought peace in that specific sense. The Pax Romana – the peace of Rome – enabled the gospel to spread. That we have a gospel and a church today, in one sense, was possible because Paul was able to travel in relative safety, because of the Roman peace. So this is slightly different: 'makes men slay each other' sounds like civil war or revolution, and this is given away by the Greek word for sword, which is actually a dagger. It was the Roman choice of weapon for close combat and was used for assassination. It was likely that Julius Caesar, for example, was assassinated with such a weapon. So I suggest that the red horse is the spirit of revolution, of civil war. And do we not see that today? Civil wars rage across the globe. And of course, in the twentieth century, red became the colour of revolution. It is also the colour of blood.

6:5–6

The third seal: a black horse —the spirit of economic injustice

Most commentaries on the Book of Revelation link this horse and rider with famine. But, again, I think John is more subtle and sophisticated. His words are too sharply pointed to allow us simply to talk of famine. Let us examine what he says: "A quart of wheat for a day's wages, and three quarts of barley for a day's wages...." A quart of wheat was reckoned to be what was needed to feed a man, and three quarts of barley enough to feed a family. So what we are talking about here is not famine, but chronic inflation. The figures that John gives here are ten times the figures that were actual in his day. In other words, the average man could not afford to feed himself and his family and have very much left over. And what about this funny little phrase: "Do not damage the oil and the wine"? It might be said that for some the oil and wine represent the little comforts, the little luxuries, in life, by which we tell ourselves that everything is really alright and that life is really quite grand. Today, what would it be? Vintage champagne and caviar? Of course we do have to remember that, in the cultural context, wine and oil were essential basic foodstuffs, as they are today in many parts of the world. Nonetheless, the passage as a whole carries an implicit rebuke, directed at the greed and materialism which was so rampant in John's society and in ours today. It is interesting to note that Domitian, emperor when John wrote, ordered a redistribution of land in AD92, passing an edict that the oil groves and the vineyards were to be ploughed up for other crops; but such was the public protest that this ruling had to be reversed. It seems that what we have here is not just plain famine, but chronic economic injustice. Of course, the long-term result of economic selfishness is famine and hardship for so many people in our world, now as then. Due to unfair distribution of our resources, the poor starve for the price of a loaf of bread – that is what John's words imply – while the better-off enjoy their luxuries. The black horse symbolises economic injustice. The scales reminded me of the scales at Belshazzar's feast— "You have been weighed on the scales and found wanting" (Daniel 5:27). Today, we might ponder the divide between the developed nations and the developing nations, between North and South; and, of course, we all love to blame different things, according to our political colour. We blame the government of the day; we blame the whole capitalist enterprise; we blame the trade unions; we blame corrupt regimes; we blame those wretched bankers; we blame the super-rich; and sometimes we even blame the poor themselves for the mess they get into. But John's real point is a bit closer to home: the real root of economic injustice is a stain on all our hands; so much of the world's poverty is caused simply because we will not let go of our materialistic expectations. We insist upon maintaining our level of lifestyle in the West, even if it means destitution for the poor and the weak elsewhere. I will enjoy my cheap coffee, even if it means backbreaking labour for countless women in the developing world. It seems to me that the black horse rides very close to home and may even have found stabling among us.

6:7–8
The fourth seal: a pale horse —death on a massive scale
The word rendered 'pale' in the NIV is in fact 'yellowy green' and was a medical term in the Greek language applied to the pallor of people who were on their last legs. We might say that someone looks like 'death warmed up' —and that is exactly what this character is. Following him is Hades, the abode of the dead. The pale horse then symbolises massive loss of life. The figures – as with so many of the figures in Revelation – are symbolic of course: 'a quarter of the world's population' – well they are symbolic, but not unrealistic, are they?

• In 1348 rats arrived in Europe bringing the plague that, within 3 to 5 years, had wiped out a third of the population of Europe.
• A fifth of the world's population, today, stands on the brink of starvation.

• A third of Africa's population is projected to die of the AIDS virus over the next 10 to 20 years.

Symbolic figures, yes; unrealistic, no. Our world today is as vulnerable as it ever was to sword, famine and plague. And what of the wild beasts that John sees accompanying the pale rider? Maybe he means the descent into savagery that almost inevitably follows the breakdown of civilisation. Think back to some of the images from Kosovo, Bosnia, or Iraq —that is not war but barbarism. The things done to women and children across the globe are not acts of war, but savagery. Savagery is the level to which humanity so quickly descends when war, famine and plague follow hard on each others' heels. The four horsemen hardly present a rosy view of our future, yet how plausible a view of the future it seems. It is amazing how many secular pessimists quote Revelation in huge chunks. When, at the end of the last century, scientists predicted that an asteroid would strike earth in the middle of this century, a major television programme devoted to considering the likely impact of such a catastrophic event quoted extensively from Revelation. We see evidence of the four horsemen everywhere we look. We open a newspaper, turn on the television —the four horsemen ride, today! How significant is it? Does it mean that we are at the End? There are certainly many Christians who believe that that is so, who join the secular pessimists in predicting unremitting doom and gloom. But is this the conclusion that John wants us to draw? Is this what John intends us to feel, as we see the horsemen ride through the pages of history?

When Jesus talked to his disciples in Matthew 24, as we saw in chapter four above, he set a pattern for everything that we read in Revelation. When the disciples asked for the signs of the Lord's coming, the first thing Jesus said was "Watch out that no-one deceives you" (v. 4). He goes on to warn there will be wars, rumours of wars, famine, revolutions, earthquakes, pestilences. He is describing the four horsemen. But he teaches that that is only the beginning; the End will not yet have come. And this raises one of the problems we noticed at the beginning of this chapter —the timing of the fulfilment of what John predicts.

From John's visions it appears that the seals were broken by Jesus. As he ascended into glory and he was received into heaven, suddenly there was one among the heavenly host who was worthy to break the seals; there was no more delay, for Christ set about breaking them. So, actually, what we looked at in Revelation 4 and 5 was looking back in John's time. We read that Jesus broke the seals and we look back to the moment of resurrection and ascension. The last days were ushered in as Jesus died, and rose again, and poured out the Spirit. The seals continue to be broken, and will be broken until the End. The four horsemen ride and always will ride until the End. At times their hoofbeats sound louder than at other times; and Christians, sadly, have often scurried to predict the End is near, when Jesus taught that it was not —the English Civil War, the Middle Ages, the turn of the first millennium, the First World War; name your period in history, and there have been those in the church who have hastened to say the End is upon us. Yet Jesus warned us that the four horsemen are but the beginnings. John's readers would have recognised the four horsemen; we recognise the four horsemen; but we should not jump to conclusions, nor become hysterical, because Jesus has told us not to be alarmed. One thing the four horsemen do signify is that any utopian dream of humanistic improvement is doomed to disappointment. Maybe the human race will survive long into the future; maybe science will conquer the great problems which we face at the moment; maybe the end of the world is still centuries away. But from John's message we learn that: our world will never find peace, will never defeat disease, will never conquer economic injustice, will never eliminate hunger or poverty, and will never beat death. The belief that utopia will be delivered through human effort is sadly mistaken. The horsemen ride. Things are not going to get better, they are going to get an awful lot worse. Just look at the number of wars and earthquakes and natural disasters there have been over the last hundred years or so, which historians and scientists tell us were more widespread than in any other period of history.

6:9–11
The fifth seal: the souls of the martyrs

According to John, the same sad state of affairs will apply to the church, as we see in the breaking of the fifth seal. The remaining optimists in the secular world – those who believe in utopia – have their counterparts within the church, just as do the secular pessimists. They believe that, largely through Christian social and spiritual action, the world will get better, Christians will actually sweep all evil from before the face of the Lord before he returns, and that Christian political action will establish true justice and economic freedom. Jonathan Edwards was a very good example of this tendency; seeing extraordinary revival in his own day, he came to believe that revival would sweep the earth. Well, it is a lovely idea, but it does not square with the Scriptures, nor with Christian experience. What does John see here? 'The souls of those who had been slain because of the word of God and the testimony they had maintained.' And that was exactly the sign that Jesus went on to talk about in Matthew 24. Worldwide persecution will become the normative experience of the church. These souls beneath the altar are crying for vengeance, like the blood of Abel centuries ago. It is not a picture of worldwide revival, is it? It is not a picture of Christian political parties establishing worldwide dominance. And what is the message for the souls of the martyrs? Wait, there is more. Wait, you are going to be joined by others. The pattern is set for the persecution of Christians down the centuries. The church was already being persecuted under Domitian. Jesus' call to take up your own cross is not, after all, a call stoically to accept minor disappointments cheerfully; nor is it a call simply to accept your rheumatism; it is a call to martyrdom. And the Romans knew how to martyr people: Christians were tied to catapults and pulled apart; put into sacks with snakes; or had their feet slowly burnt away while cold water was poured on them to stop them dying too quickly. Jesus' words are clear: those who seek to follow Jesus and to remain faithful cannot expect to avoid persecution; and our brothers and sisters in the Soviet countries of old suffered, and in many other territories even today still suffer, as martyrs. We have grown comfortable in the West. We think that, because we have had two centuries of relative religious tolerance, that is normative. In fact, the Bible shows us that it is abnormal.

6:12–17
The sixth seal: convulsions in the cosmos

What we might term John's 'pessimism' now reaches its climax, with a glimpse of the very far future. Again, notice how John's vision follows precisely the pattern laid down by Jesus in Matthew 24. Here, John moves beyond our present experience to something we cannot even imagine. It is definitely the end of the age (verse 17) 'for the great day of [their] wrath has come.' In Matthew 24:29–30, Jesus refers to cosmic distress, adding: 'At that time, the Son of Man will appear'. There is a direct chronological link between cosmic distress and the return of Christ. Peter writes, 'The heavens will disappear with a roar; the elements will be destroyed by fire, and the earth and everything in it will be laid bare' (See 2 Peter 3:10). The author of Hebrews writes, 'You will roll them up like a robe; like a garment they will be changed' (1:12). In Isaiah 34:4 we read that,

> All the stars of the heavens will be dissolved
> and the sky rolled up like a scroll;
> all the starry hosts will fall
> like withered leaves from the vine,
> like shrivelled figs from the fig-tree.

The words of Isaiah, Jesus himself and John are conveying a message to us: learn the lesson of the fig tree. And why are we told all this? Because such cosmic collapse will cause terror. Look at verses 16f: everybody is scuttling for cover which does not exist. This is a day of absolute terror, when rank means nothing —princes and slaves alike run for cover. The classless society will finally have come about, though not quite as Marx thought it would. Remember that this is all foreshadowed in the Old Testament. Isaiah prophesies exactly this sort of behaviour from the inhabitants of the earth (2:10, 19 & 21).

We are introduced to a paradox here: 'The wrath of the Lamb'. How can a lamb be wrathful? How can one whose heart was so full of love that he gave his life also exercise righteous anger? We are told today, so often, that the wrath of God is not acceptable, that it is some simplistic mediaeval superstition which we can well do without. Yet the Bible will insist that God's wrath is a fundamental aspect of his character, without which his love would be just so much sentimentality. And if God does not come to judge the earth, then the new world for which we long and wait will hardly be a great deal better than the semi-hell we inhabit now. What a prospect, to behold the face of him who sits on the throne! Who can stand? Can you —in the day when the stars fall and the world implodes, when your social status means nothing, when your hard-earned wealth means nothing, when your lovely home and your high-powered job mean nothing, when everything by which you are regarded and esteemed in life means nothing? No secrets will remain hidden on that day. Nothing you have done in darkness will avoid being revealed in light. Nothing you have whispered in the dark corners of your heart will not be played back in stereo, full volume. Compare Jesus' words in Luke 12, and consider: who can stand?

Chapter 7 —the first insertion

We can see why Chapter 7 is placed where it is by John —because it answers the question 'who can stand?' The pause between the 6th and 7th seals introduces us to two companies of people. We now move from pessimism to optimism. We now begin to see earth history from the heavenly perspective, and we are introduced to four angels standing at the four corners of the earth. I believe they are the four horsemen of the apocalypse again. And they are clearly standing ready to do damage. Yet now they are not riding forth, they are being held back. Why? —because God wants his servants to be sealed. In the ancient world, a seal was a sign of three things:

1. ownership
2. authenticity
3. inviolability —in other words they cannot be harmed.

So God is making it clear concerning his people:

1. they are mine
2. they are real
3. they are not to be touched.

The vital question is, of course, 'Who are they?' There are so many different views. If the 144,000 which we read of first are really the faithful remnant of the Jews, then the tribe of Dan is a bit unfortunate, because it is missed out, replaced by the tribe of Manasseh. Possibly that is because Dan in Judges 18:30 was very closely associated with idolatry and evil. Maybe Dan is an Old Testament foreshadowing of Judas, who lost his place among the apostles? And then, what of this great multitude: is it possible that they are the same group of people? Notice that in verse 4 he hears the number, and then in verse 9 he looks and he sees. I see here a symbolic representation of God's faithful people, on earth sealed, in glory resplendent —all those who have stood firm in the face of persecution over the ages; in the face of the carnage of the four horsemen throughout history; and finally in the face of that terrible day when everything will collapse. The good news is that if we are Christ's we are sealed. We are marked with a seal. God knows his people. In John 10, the Gospel records Jesus saying, "I am the good shepherd", and "I know my sheep"; Paul writes to the Ephesians that, 'Having believed, you were marked in him [Christ] with a seal, the promised Holy Spirit, who is a deposit guaranteeing our inheritance until the redemption of those who are God's possession...' (1:13f.) It is wonderful to know that Christ knows us, that he has marked us as his. Jesus himself told us not to fear those who destroy the body, but rather the one who can destroy the soul in hell. We are not to fear the horsemen of the apocalypse. We are not to fear God's judgment upon the earth, because our lives are hid in Christ. In John 6:39, Jesus says, "And this is the will of him who sent me, that I shall lose none of all that he has given me, but raise them up at the last day." That is God's will for you, if you are a Christian. And Paul is confident, in Romans 8, that nothing can separate us from that love. This multitude – they have white robes signifying they are forgiven – are pure. And who are they? They are those who have 'come out' of the great tribulation (v. 14) —not escaped from it, note; there is no hint of a secret rapture here. They have gone through the tribulation; they have gone through the days of the horsemen. They have come through and they have been redeemed, a multitude without number. Both groups, on earth and in heaven, are complete; for all those who are sealed with the Spirit of God in this life receive promotion into glory. And note that being in heaven is a foretaste of the new heaven and the new earth. When John records the wonderful promise of verse 15, that 'he who sits on the throne will spread his tent over them', how that must have resonated with his Jewish readers, who would think of the Book of Ruth, when Boaz pledges his love and protection for her by spreading his cloak over her. And what a reward awaits those who are faithful. 'Never again will they hunger; never again will they thirst.' This is our destiny. Isn't it glorious! —never to hunger, never to thirst, never to feel the scorching heat. And then there is another paradox. 'The Lamb at the centre of the throne will be their shepherd; he will lead them to springs of living water.' What echoes of Psalm 23 and John 10, where the Bible describes the Lord as our shepherd, guiding and protecting us along life's way.

Although we have dismissed the idea of a utopian world fashioned by human endeavour and technological advance, we do have a glorious hope given to us by God. We must accept and proclaim both the grim truth about this world's future, and also the hope of the future in God, if we are to be true Christian realists. We balance the 'pessimism' that would naturally flow from awareness of the state of our world, with the perspective of heaven. On the day when St Augustine heard that Rome had been sacked by the barbarians, he preached to an anxious congregation, in the following words: 'There will be an end to every earthly kingdom. This world is passing away. This world is short of breath. But do not fear, your youth shall be renewed, as the eagle's.'

8:1–5
The seventh seal: silence in heaven

And lest we fear that there is no bridge between the desperate state of life here and its future on the one hand, and the hope of heaven on the other, a 7th seal is broken. And what an astonishing effect it has! If you have read Revelation right the way through to this point, you will have an image of incredible noise, whether it is the terror and fear of earth, as people run hither and thither, looking for cover; whether it is the sound of earthquakes, wars, rumours of wars, plague; or whether it is the praises of heaven, the voices loud as trumpets, the sound of waterfalls, the praises of thousands upon thousands of angels, the four living creatures, the twenty-four elders. You have an example of the praise in chapter 7 —'Praise and glory and wisdom and thanks and honour and power and strength...' (See v. 12.) You know already how important sequence of sevens are, and here is sevenfold praise, perfect praise of God. And every creature in heaven falls over. And yet, chapter 8 opens with silence in heaven for about half an hour. That John manages to note the length of the silence strikes me as one of the most poignantly human touches in the whole of the book. The reason for this silence in heaven is to listen to our prayers, so that, mingled with the incense presented on the altar in front of God's temple and before the throne, they can be heard. It is the most astonishing thing, that heaven holds its breath to catch the prayers of the saints

—and that is the bridge between the two worlds. Prayer is the means by which we offer to God all we see and feel, as we look around our world. Prayer is the bridge by which we bring to God those things which are the result of the riding forth of the horsemen. And prayer is the bridge by which we receive the heavenly perspective on the world in which we live. We do not have to be governed in our thinking of the future by our newspapers and our television, because we have God's perspective on the pages of human history. We must become more and more prayerful individuals, and more and more a prayerful church, because prayer is the bridge between earth and heaven, by which we gain realism and the strength to stand.

We cannot afford to be complacent. The four horsemen ride to great effect. They do their grim work well today. And individual crises, or groups of crises, will pass, but they will come again, with increasing severity, as human history winds up, as the story of men and women coils itself ever more tightly around tragedy and cruelty, until the day when the stars fall and the world falls apart and the inhabitants of earth quake with terror. And on that day there will only be one place of safety; there will only be one group of people who can, without fainting from terror, behold him who sits on the throne —one group of people who will be able to look into the eyes of the Lamb. Are you one of them?

Heavenly Father, in your word, we are encouraged to make our calling and our election certain. Father, we pray for friends who do not know the certainty of your calling upon their lives, who do not know that they will be able to stand on the day of the Lamb. Father, by your Spirit, enable them to place their trust in you, to become part of that great multitude without number, who one day will join you around the throne to sing your praises and to share in the new heaven and the new earth. In Jesus' name we pray. Amen.

7

MORE TROUBLES UPON EARTH

Revelation 8:6 – 11:19 & 15 – 16

The problem of the silence in heaven

Imagine for a moment that you are at a great musical event – perhaps a concert, an opera, or maybe the last night of the proms – and the music is building to the crescendo. You do not know the piece of music particularly well, but you can tell that it is coming to an end, because the music is building all the time. You know that it is soon to end. Sooner or later you get to that moment where the conductor raises his hands for the final bars —and then nothing happens! Or again, imagine for a moment the scene at one of the great open air gatherings on New Year's Eve 1999. The crowd around you hushes as the two hands meet at twelve o'clock, and you wait for the first booming chime to signal midnight, new year, new century, new millennium —and nothing happens.

It is rather like that in Revelation chapter 8. We saw that, in one sense, the silence was positive, because the prayers of the saints were a way of bridging the gloom and distress and despair of this world and the biblical hope of the world to come. But, in terms of the structure of the Book of Revelation and how we understand it, the silence is a real problem. Let us recap. The six seals in chapter 6, you remember, brought us to the very climax of human history, the very threshold of the End. The 6th seal was, itself, the cosmic convulsions which Jesus told his disciples, in Matthew 24, would signal the very End. At that time, Jesus taught, we will see the Son of Man. (See Matthew 24:30). So the 7th seal must be the End. But John, you recall, does not even go to the breaking of the 7th seal straightaway. Instead, he shifts the camera focus in chapter 7, we are taken up into heaven and we see the sealed multitude and the multitude without number. Then, even when the 7th seal is broken at the beginning of chapter 8, having had a whole chapter inserted between them, there is this strange anti-climax of the silence in heaven. The seal is broken, the stage is, seemingly, set; and yet —nothing! To return to our metaphor of a dramatic production —though always remember that what we are dealing with is reality, not performance; the truth; not fiction – it is as though someone has forgotten a cue. In a drama, the silence of embarrassment would descend upon the audience. Instead of the final crashing bars of human history, there appears to be silence. Those of us who are well-versed in Paul's writings, especially Thessalonians, are sitting back, waiting for the final trumpet.

What does John do? He introduces seven trumpets, being blown by seven angels. What is more, they are not even sounded together, but one after another. It is like going back to the seven seals all over again. Even when we get to the 6th trumpet, and everyone is on tenterhooks again at the end of chapter 9, the whole feeling of anti-climax is repeated: there is another interlude (chapters 10 and 11). Then, when the 7th trumpet is finally sounded at the end of chapter 11, there is not a silence, but another insertion (chapters 12 to 14). After this, we are introduced again to a set of seven angels – and this time the seven angels have seven bowls full of plagues or wrath. Yet even this does not signal the End because, after the 7th bowl is poured out, there is yet another insertion (chapters 17 and 18) before finally – no doubt with a good sense of relief, at least for John, if not for us – Jesus rides forth on the white horse.

So the End has been glimpsed, and in some cases detailed, on several occasions, before we get there. Remember the image of being on a roller coaster ride through a gallery hung with impressionist art. At each twist and turn you get a different glimpse of the future —sometimes behind you, sometimes beside you, sometimes still way ahead.

A comparison of seals, trumpets and bowls

The problem of the silence in heaven is fundamental to the understanding of the book and its structure. We have already noted that the book is built around series of sevens: 7 churches, 7 seals, 7 bowls, 7 trumpets, 7 angels, and so on; and so I want to compare the seals, the trumpets and the bowls. Please refer to the chart on page 90 as you read on.

We have looked in detail at the seals already, but you will see there that each series divides into three.

1. The first four in each series are a set: for the seals, four horsemen; for the trumpets and the bowls, they are identical —earth, seas, rivers and sun.

2. The fifth and sixth are not so closely related, but they move us from the earthly realm into some spiritual sphere, either divine or demonic.

3. The seventh then stands alone: a cataclysm; cosmic convulsion.

You will notice that John is already beginning to develop one particular piece of shorthand —namely the word 'earthquake', which when you see it in the Book of Revelation is John's shorthand way of saying this is it; this is the End. So just let us look at those instances. It may help you, if you don't find this too confusing, to have a finger in chapters 8 and 9 and a finger in chapter 16 of Revelation; and we will briefly look at the trumpets and the bowls.

The first trumpet (8:7) and the first bowl (16:2)

Hail, fire and blood, we read in 8:7; and ugly and painful sores in 16:2. The common thing is that they are poured out upon the earth and upon the inhabitants of earth. Straightaway, for those of us who know our Old Testament, we are right back in the plagues of Egypt —specifically, the 7th plague (the 1st trumpet) and the 6th plague (the 1st bowl). You can read about them in Exodus 7 to 11.

The second trumpet (8:8–9) and the second bowl (16:3)
Both recall the first plague on Egypt —the sea turned to blood.

The third trumpet (8:10) and the third bowl (16:4)
These deal with the rivers and springs. Having dealt with the salt water of the planet, we are now into the fresh water. In Revelation 8, we read of a star, Wormwood. Wormwood is a plant, with a very strong and very bitter taste; and, all the way through the Old Testament, it is used as a metaphor for calamity and sorrow. It occurs in Proverbs, in Jeremiah and in Lamentations —to name only three examples. Notice also that it is the reverse of one of the miracles wrought by Moses in the desert —the miracle at the waters of Marah in Exodus 15:23, where Moses turned bitter water sweet. Here fresh spring water is turned bitter. Again, we note John's use of the imagery of the Exodus.

In 16:4–7 (the third bowl), we are again reminded of the plagues. In verse 5 the divine name is used —again from Exodus and, as we have already seen, that name for God is significant throughout the Book of Revelation. It would seem that this bowl is a specific punishment to the earth, specifically related to the killing of the saints. In other words, you might say, God is making clear in vivid pictorial language that the punishment fits the crime. This is terrifying imagery, startlingly vivid, but it is confirmed when we consider Babylon in chapters 17 and 18. One of the characteristics of Babylon – which symbolises human rebellion against God – is that it is drunk with the blood of the saints.

The fourth trumpet (8:12) and the fourth bowl (16:8)
These affect the sun, moon and stars —the source of light is attacked. The 9th plague of Egypt, again. This constant reference to the initial Exodus of God's people suggests to

me that one of the themes that is being revealed in this series of John's visions, is that the end of all things will finally see God's people set free; finally brought out from being bound to a world of evil and sin. This will be the exodus to end all exoduses.

In chapter 16, the sun scorches people. Throughout the Bible, fire is often a sign of God's judgment. How plausible these predictions are. We know that human beings could quite easily unleash ecological devastation and pollution upon the face of the planet, whether by design or terrible accident. One of the modern scientific scenarios for the end of life on planet earth is simply that the earth will be drawn nearer to the sun, so that everything will be burnt up. Today, few scientists can be found upon the face of the planet who believe anything other than that planet earth is heading to its end. They disagree about how it will get there, but they are in total agreement that the lifespan of this planet is finite —and that is quite a shift in scientific thinking over recent decades.

But notice also that people will still not repent (16:9). They continue to curse God.

The fifth trumpet (9:1–12) and the fifth bowl (16:10)

Whereas the fifth seal moved us from the sphere of earth into the presence of God and the great multitude around the throne, the fifth trumpet and the fifth bowl both take us down —into the depths of the demonic dwellings, the abyss or the throne of the beast. Chapter 9 increasingly becomes the stuff of nightmares —the demonic interplay with human life. The fallen star is almost certainly Satan, because it is common elsewhere in Scripture for his downfall to be described in this way, beginning with Isaiah 14:12. In Luke 10:18, Jesus says that he saw Satan fall from heaven. In Revelation 12, there is a description of war in heaven, and Satan is thrown down. The abyss, for the Hebrews and the early church, was the abode of demons. The expression occurs in Luke 8:31. The literal meaning of the Greek is simply 'bottomless'. Out of this abyss come weird creatures that look like locusts. Again,

John is steeped in the imagery of the Old Testament, drawing in particular from the Book of Exodus and the Book of Joel. Locusts were one of the plagues upon ancient Egypt (Exodus 10); Joel interpreted an attack of locusts in his day as foreshadowing the devastation of the planet, which would accompany the coming Day of the Lord. The only glimmer of hope, here in chapter 9 of Revelation, is the limited power and duration of this demonic activity (verses 4, 5 & 10). Limits are set both for the damage that will be done and for how long the damage can be done.

God is still sovereign. Notice that the first woe, as this is called in Revelation 9, does not fall on God's people, but on the inhabitants of earth. We are reminded of the protection afforded to the Israelites in the first exodus, when the plagues were falling upon Egypt. In 9:6 we are told that people will seek death but not find it. A Roman poet called Cornelius Garrus, writing in the first century BC, wrote, 'Worse than any wound, is to wish to die and yet not be able to do so.' What a contrast with Paul's attitude to death – which should be ours – that you can read about in Philippians 1:21, 'For to me... to die is gain.'

When the locusts begin to appear as something like scorpions, this gives us a hint that we are dealing with the occult here. Initially, the appearance is deceptively beautiful. The occult often seems wonderful. People dabble in it because they think it will give them power or an exciting trip. But there is an enormous sting in the tail, lurking behind the face and the hair of beauty —because these things are led by the king of the abyss, Abaddon, or Apollyon. These are simply the Hebrew and Greek words for 'the destroyer'. Notice how John is at pains to paint Satan as infinitely weaker than God. There is no comparison. God can draw the cosmos into being simply by speaking the word. All Satan can do is destroy. There is no creativity in Satan; there is no life in Satan —it is destruction and death all the way. We ought also to note, in passing, that Satan – unlike God – is not able to be everywhere at once. He can exercise influence through his minions, the fallen angels; he can gain influence over us as we submit to him in sin —which is why we have the lists here of the sins of the people.

In chapter 16:10–11, we see the throne of the beast. Again, John is at pains to emphasise the distinction between God and Satan —the word 'throne' occurs 42 times in the Book of Revelation, but only here and in Revelation 2 does it refer to Satan's throne. The other 40 instances all refer to God's throne. What an emphasis John is making on the majesty and greatness of God, unlike his enemy. Yet, again, you will find here (6:11) that people still curse and refuse to repent. The irony of this is emphasised by John's taking up Daniel's great attribute of God —the God of heaven (remember in Daniel 2:44, that is the phrase that is used to describe the God he serves), the God of all majesty, the God of all creative power, is the one who is being refused submission here.

The sixth trumpet (9:13) and sixth bowl (16:12)

These have the River Euphrates in common. In 9:13f we are introduced again to four angels. I believe they are most likely to be the same four angels that we found bound at the beginning of chapter 7. Notice how similar the description of the forces they unleash here in chapter 9 is to the description of the locusts. Again, there is no repentance; and the list of evil acts once more emphasises Satan's power acquired through our sin. The sixth bowl is again a demonic thing, the evil spirits. We must beware of being deceived, because these demons are able to perform miracles, which is another of the signs that Jesus taught his disciples to watch for in Matthew 24. But do note the fundamental purpose of demonic activity is revealed here in chapter 16, as they gather the kings of the world for battle against God. John is telling us that the ultimate aim of demonic activity is to inspire, to strengthen, and to nurture rebellion in humans against God. Potentially, all human beings are capable of such rebellion, and Satan's work is to foster it. Satan wants to sign you up to the kings of the earth who are going to do battle against God.

The seventh trumpet (11:15), the seventh bowl (16:17)

Again, just as with the 7th seal, we are expecting the End, because the proclamations begin to peal out from the heavenly realms. In 11:15 we hear loud voices proclaiming, "The kingdom of the world has become the kingdom of our Lord and of his Christ, and he will reign for ever and ever." In 11:17 we find an interesting description of God as "the One who is and who was" —no longer one who is to come. That does not need to be said any more, because God has come. The Lord's Prayer is redundant, for the kingdom has arrived, and God's will shall be done on earth as in heaven. He has begun to reign. God does not have to be called 'who is to come' anymore, because he is here; this is the End. Note that the nations were still angry, reminding us of Psalm 2:1f.

> Why do the nations conspire
> and the peoples plot in vain?
> The kings of the earth take their stand
> and the rulers gather together against the LORD
> and his Anointed One.

The time has come for the judging of the dead, the rewarding of the saints and for destroying those who destroy the earth. Here is another hint that the trumpets, the bowls and the seals are, in large part, the result of human sin and error. The heavenly temple is opened and, yet again, the shorthand of John —the earthquake.

In 16:17–21, the voice from the temple says, "It is done!" Those words remind me of Jesus' words on the cross, "It is finished." We find it again in chapter 16, the seventh bowl: the earthquake —nothing like it. The great city is split apart, the nations of the earth begin to fall —that is the End. Some say the 'great city' is Jerusalem, but I do not think it is. I think it is Babylon, again the symbol of human rebellion. That appears to be confirmed in 17:18, when Babylon is specifically identified as the great city.

So, clearly, there are great similarities between the trumpets and the bowls; and it is chilling to realise how, through our own greed, folly and carelessness, we face a very possible outworking of those judgments. Yet we still have to decide how we understand these series of sevens, within the context of the book. They so clearly portray the same events over and over again, as our roller coaster dips and weaves and bends, revealing first this view, and then that view. How do we understand it? Is there a pattern whereby we can fit these chapters into a framework that actually works? Two main suggestions have been made.

The first, and this is predominantly the understanding across the American evangelical church at the moment, is this: you start reading the Book of Revelation, and its events unfold in a literal sequence. So you have firstly seals, then trumpets, then bowls. Now most popular books – and I guess the most famous recent one is the series of novels under the title 'Left Behind' – are a very good read, but I do want to sound a cautionary note about one aspect of them in particular. They see Revelation as a timeline, a chart by which we can determine what is going to happen next. There are huge problems with this way of seeing it. For a start, we have already seen that the 7th seal, the 7th trumpet and the 7th bowl are all referring to the same event. So how does that fit into a linear sequence? If you wanted to be really pedantic, you might ask: How can the sun, moon and stars turn dark in chapter 8 when they have already turned dark, to blood, and fallen from the sky in chapter 6? How can the beast attack and kill the two witnesses in chapter 11, when he does not even appear until chapter 13? I suggest that Revelation 6 to 18 will not follow a precise chronological sequence. I suggest that you simply cannot read the Book of Revelation as a time chart —either of the whole of earth history, or any particular part of it.

So what, then, is the solution? I have already suggested that the imagery of Revelation is not necessarily always to be taken literally. I would like to suggest that the chronology also falls into the same mould. There is another, more ancient church view of the Book of Revelation and the end of the world, which is still held by many today and is probably the most popular in Europe: it sees a simultaneous, or cyclical, pattern for the Book of Revelation. This avoids the problems of the linear view. Each of the series of sevens, together with their various insertions, covers part of the whole of earth history, the present age —the time between the ascension of Jesus and his return. This does not rule out the likelihood that the events pictured in the seals, the trumpets and the bowls, will greatly intensify in severity as the End draws near. Indeed the language of these chapters suggests precisely that: trumpets 2 and 3 affect a third of the sea and the rivers and springs, and yet bowls 2 and 3 affect the whole of them —so there is clearly an understanding that the intensity and the severity worsen. But this view does avoid the problems of trying to force a chronological sequence onto material obviously unwilling to wear it. Is that not the problem always with a straitjacket —that people are not willing to wear it? Consider one little example from 10:6f. We hear the voice of an angel saying, "There will be no more delay." The 7th trumpet will lead to the accomplishment of God's purposes; and yet, after the 7th trumpet, we have to wait another seven chapters before those purposes are, indeed, accomplished. And the cyclical view has one great advantage: it provides a pattern, which covers the whole of this middle section of the Book of Revelation and avoids the problems of the earlier model.

I want to emphasise again that John is not concerned to give us a time chart but, rather, to communicate the way in which history in the last days will move through cycles of increasingly intense disruption, tribulation and judgment, with periods of respite in between. Do not try to work out which seal, or trumpet, or bowl we have reached in human history. John is, as it were, creating within us the emotional suspense that corresponds to the mounting tension of world events as the End draws near. So, in these middle chapters of Revelation, the visions swing between different viewpoints in earth and in heaven, showing us the same events, the same characters, the same futures —first far off, then near, then to the side, then behind.

For example, God's people are seen by God, they are seen by Satan and they are seen by the inhabitants of the earth. The inhabitants of the earth are seen in various images, which reveal their religious, political, and economic alliances with the enemy. Satan himself is seen as he appears to the inhabitants of the earth, to God's people and to God. These visions are not intended to fit any date or time sequence which humans might dream up. John is not concerned to give us a schematic for earth's last days, as some writers suggest, but rather to provide a pattern by which we may understand our call to be faithful followers of Christ, against the backdrop of the reality of evil, here and now, and the certainty of Christ's return. John's visions explain these realities in vivid form, in order that we might show patient endurance and faithfulness (13:10). The future is only ever unveiled in order to transform the present.

It seems to me that those who try to force the Book of Revelation into a form which simply moves from A to B miss the point of the book. It is not that John is not interested in specific fulfilment —he clearly is, and he sees specific fulfilment coming again and again. But that is because history, in a certain sense, does repeat itself, if not exactly. If, for John's day, the emperor was identified as the beast, then in every age the church should be able to identify beasts. Just as the Old Testament prophets saw in the great clash of the ancient superpowers, Egypt, Babylon and Assyria, and the fate of Israel caught between them, foreshadowings of the coming of the Messiah, so John sees in the political, religious and social events of his own day, foreshadowings of the end of all things.

This does not mean that we rule out specific fulfilment of specific individual characters in the Book of Revelation at the very End, but we do not limit ourselves to them. Again, John's revelations are like a series of impressionist portraits of the way history goes. That makes a big difference to the way in which we interpret the characters and the events that we meet within its pages.

If we adopt the system I am proposing, we are able to discern a detailed pattern in the Book of Revelation chapters 6 to 18, which has four main themes: God's activity in judgment and mercy; Satan's activity in wrath and deception; the fate of the earth; the fate of God's people.

John's primary purpose is not to enable us to gather in our little excited huddles, plotting over dates and charts, and getting all worked up and, quite frankly, to no earthly purpose. Rather, the purpose is to enable us to be faithful followers of Christ, ready to face the worst that can come our way. You might ask, if the great tribulation is only going to occupy a very short period – some will say seven years – at the end of earth's history, why we should 'waste' our time preparing for it now. There are two very good reasons why you should 'waste your time' preparing for it now. Firstly, you do not know whether or not you are in the last generation, whether you are going to be alive in those seven years; and, secondly, the future, theologically, always casts its shadow ahead of it. There are always foreshadowings now of what is to come. Any Christian, anywhere, can go through tribulations, before we all go through tribulation —those of us who are left. John, himself, writing his first letter said, 'This is the last hour, and already many antichrists have gone out among you.' The major false prophet, yes, is still to come. The major beast is still yet to come. Yet, in a sense, they are here now. In other words, what will one day be experienced by all believers can be experienced now on a local scale. So these chapters are directly relevant to us all. Remember that the main motive for preparing us to be faithful and loyal servants of Jesus, here on earth, is that when that day comes, we may behold the One who sits on the throne, that we may look into the face of the Lamb, without fear or shame.

We conclude this chapter with just one verse that echoes Jesus' own words of warning from Matthew 24. "Behold, I come like a thief! Blessed is he who stays awake and keeps his clothes with him, so that he may not go naked and be shamefully exposed" (16:15). We are reminded of the promise of white robes for the martyrs, the white robes of the faithful, which symbolize the purifying works of the Spirit, once we have placed our trust in the redemptive work of Christ.

But Jesus told a very sobering parable in Matthew 22 —the parable of the wedding banquet. He pictures a scene where everything is ready, all is prepared to receive the bride and groom, all the guests are present. Then the stewards notice that someone has sneaked in uninvited, and without the necessary wedding clothes —and is thrown out. How well are you dressed today?

Heavenly Father, we thank you for the great encouragement of this book —even though, in parts, it seems hard to understand. Lord, we thank you for the great vision of heaven opened; and we pray that in dark days that vision of you, seated upon your throne in majesty, surrounded by those who have gone ahead of us in faith, may sustain us and encourage us. We pray that our increasing knowledge of what you have revealed about what is to come will strengthen us to be faithful and to stand. Lord, we pray that whether we are to remain until you come, or whether we shall die and come with you in glory, you will now confirm to us your gift of grace; that you will make us sure of our calling in you; that you will settle in our hearts that glorious rest and knowledge that we are yours. Increase in us endurance and patient faithfulness. In Jesus' name we pray. Amen.

8

CHARACTERS IN THE DRAMA
Revelation 11–14

The two witnesses of Revelation 11 are a major focus for speculation among popularists and controversy among scholars. Are we to expect two historical figures to walk the streets of Jerusalem as the days of our planet draw to their close? Are they really going to be Moses (who was able to call fire to destroy his enemies) and Elijah (for whom God prevented rain falling from the heavens)?

The chapter begins with John being handed the equivalent of a surveyor's tape measure and told to measure 'the temple of God and the altar, and count the worshippers there.' He is told not to include the outer court, as 'it has been given to the Gentiles [who] will trample on the holy city for 42 months.' There may be an intentional reference here to Psalm 79:1. Some commentators find the background for this period in the time of Jewish suffering under the Syrian tyrant, Antiochus Epiphanes (168 – 165 BC), though his desecration of the temple lasted only three years, not three and a half. This figure certainly looks back to the dividing of the 70th 'seven' of Daniel 9:27 into two equal parts. The same time period is also designated as 1260 days (v. 3 & 12:6 —note these are months of 30 days), and also as 'a time, times and half a time.'(See 12:14; Daniel 7:25; 12:7). This period of time became a conventional symbol for a limited period of unrestrained wickedness. We will return to this timespan in a later chapter.

What can we learn about the two witnesses from the text?

• They will be given power by God (a characteristic mark of the servants of God, especially the Old Testament prophets).

• They will prophesy for 1260 days (42 months, the same timespan given for Gentile defiling of the temple).

• They are described as 'the two olive trees and the two lampstands' that stand before the Lord of the earth.

• They are initially invincible against attack.

• They have supernatural powers —to send forth devouring fire; to stop the rain; to turn waters to blood and to inflict any plague at will [recalling Elijah's power to call forth fire from heaven (see 1 Kings 1:10, 12; 1 Kings 18:38) ; the drought in Elijah's day (1 Kings 17:1; see also Luke 4:25 & James 5:17); the plague of Exodus 7:17–21].

• At the end of their allotted time of testimony, the beast from the Abyss will kill them (and the text makes clear that this happens in Jerusalem '...where also their Lord was crucified').

• They will then be supernaturally resurrected and will ascend into heaven.

Well, we may be looking for two historical characters to bear testimony, in Jerusalem, before the world ends. I am sure that, if we are to see them, then we will know them when we do. But we must beware any suggestion that this passage implies reincarnation, and there is no justification within the text for saying that these are literally Moses and Elijah brought back to life. When Jesus talked of John the Baptist and said 'John is Elijah', he was clearly talking of a type of prophetic figure.

It seems to me that the real significance of these two characters is what they do and what is done to them. Maybe there will be two individuals who walk the streets of Jerusalem at the end of all time; but it seems to me that they speak to us of the present age as well. And I think that is given away by the fact that they are referred to as 'lampstands' here. In Revelation 1:20 we learnt that 'lampstands' are a symbol of communities of believers. I take it that these two witnesses, inasmuch as they represent anything in the present age, before the very End, are most likely to be the church and believing Israel (the remnant that Paul talked about in Romans 11). And there is a very strong hint here – and we will come back to these points again and again – that, during the very last days, organised Christianity will be crushed. In 11:7 the beast (making his first appearance in the text of Revelation) defeats and kills the two witnesses. Their bodies lie in the streets for a symbolic figurative 3½ days. In the ancient Near East the denial of burial was a flagrant violation of decency. It may well be that one day the nations of the world will gloat over their success in extinguishing (as they think) Christian witness. But the world will be staggered when the church is raised to life again. And notice that it is at that very hour that the earthquake, which we already know means the End, happens. Again, John is telling us that these are events right at the end of time.

CHAPTERS 12–13

These chapters of Revelation introduce us to three of the main characters of the book; and they appear as an unholy trio. We meet them in the form of a dragon and two beasts. In 12:3, we meet the first one, the dragon, a red dragon, who, we are told in verse 9, is none other than Satan, the devil and – in a reference back to Eden and the start of the whole sorry story of human sin – that ancient serpent. All three appear together later in 16:13, where they are described as the dragon, the beast and the false prophet.

Chapter 12:1–13:1
The woman, her child and the dragon

It is easy to identify the dragon. The text does that for us, as we have noted. We are told that he sets himself in opposition to the woman and her child; that he plans to devour the child, but is thwarted. But the identity of this woman and her child is the cause of widespread disagreement amongst commentators. There seem to be three major theories:

1. The woman is Mary, the child Jesus
2. The woman is Israel, the child Jesus
3. The woman is the church in the End times, the child restored Israel.

Let us tackle the text, verse by verse, and see what we learn.

v. 1. The woman appears 'in heaven' (a 'great and wondrous sign'). She is 'clothed with the sun, with the moon under her feet and a crown of twelve stars on her head'. Then we learn that she is in the late stages of pregnancy and in pain. In v. 5, she gives birth to a male child. In v. 6 she flees 'into the desert to a place prepared for her by God, where she might be taken care of for 1260 days.' In v. 13 she is pursued by the dragon. In v. 14, in a reference back to verse 6, we learn that her escape was supernatural. In 15f., still the dragon (now called a serpent) attacks, but again supernatural intervention ensures her safety. In v. 17, enraged at being thwarted, the dragon turns his devilish attention on the rest of her offspring who are specifically identified as, '...those who obey God's commandments and hold to the testimony of Jesus.'

Let us consider them in turn. We notice firstly that the woman is clothed with the sun, with the moon under her feet, and a crown of twelve stars on her head. She is pregnant and she gives birth to a son who will rule all the nations with an iron sceptre and who, then, is snatched up to heaven.

On this basis, many commentators – especially before the Reformation – and, indeed, most Roman Catholic commentators today, identify the woman as Mary, and the child as Jesus. This does not convince me —not least because Mary completely fades from the picture of New Testament writing, from Acts 1 onwards. It does not seem to make much sense. Moreover, the woman that John sees is in heaven; and we have already noted that it is significant when John makes those distinctions.

Many Protestant writers refer to the woman as Israel —perhaps to stop the Roman Catholics having her as Mary! There are other clues —for example, the crown of twelve stars is supposed to refer to the twelve tribes of Israel, and therefore it is suggested that here we see Israel 'giving birth' to Messiah. The pain that the woman experiences in verse 2 is described by a very similar word to that used by Isaiah in chapter 66, of the rebirth of Jerusalem —so, again, that is another little hint that some people take. Scholars agree that the child is Jesus, mainly because of the reference to ruling the nations with an iron sceptre. This is a quotation from Psalm 2:9 —one of the Messianic psalms, which was used to point ahead to the coming Messiah. Hence, say the scholars, this must refer to Jesus. But the problem I have with identifying this son with Jesus is the reference to the fact that he was snatched up to God in heaven. Some say that is a reference to the ascension, but if so it would look like a fairly untidy reference to the ascension; and, given that it is John who is writing here, John who lived with Jesus and actually saw the crucifixion, who witnessed the resurrection, and who saw the outpouring of the Holy Spirit at Pentecost, why then is there no reference to Christ's death and resurrection? It seems to me highly unlikely that one of the apostles would refer to Christ in this way.

One of the more modern and rather interesting theories is that the woman represents the church in the last days of human history; and the son, to whom the woman gives birth, is believing Israel, this 'remnant' from Romans 11, who will come in. It is an interesting theory, but it seems to me that it does not really do justice to Paul's theology in Romans, Galatians and also in Ephesians, where he really says that the gospel breaks down the barriers, that there is no need any longer to distinguish Jew and Gentile, because, in Christ, all are one. This reaches its climax in Ephesians 2, with all the teaching that Paul gives on the one new man, the one new being, the new creation. So it seemed to me that I needed to find a different explanation. The reference to the iron sceptre does come from Psalm 2:9; but actually there is another reference to it earlier in Revelation and it seems to me logical that that allusion – given that John has used it elsewhere – is going to help us more than one from a psalm. Back in Revelation 2:27, ruling with the iron sceptre is a characteristic of the saints of God —the people of God in their resurrected state. Paul writes to the Corinthians: 'Do you not know that the saints will judge the world' (1 Corinthians 6:2). So I think that this woman and child are in fact a continuation of John's teaching from chapter 11 (the two witnesses symbolising God's people); the woman and child are both symbolic representations of God's people —the woman possibly a representation of the church as an institution, and the son a representation of the individual believers. Then it makes sense, as we look through history, because God's people are always under threat. Satan is always attempting to devour them. Think of 1 Peter 5:8. The devil 'prowls around like a roaring lion looking for someone to devour.' (The same language is used here for the devil devouring the people of God). Both here, and in the case of the two witnesses, this strange figure of 1,260 days comes up. Taken together, the narrative concerning the two witnesses, and now the woman and the child, suggest that a period of intense persecution upon God's people will accompany the very end of earth history, and that during that period all organised Christian witness will disappear. The church as an institution will cease to exist, believers will be driven underground —as they have been in so many countries today. The flight of the woman to the desert suggests a measure of protection for God's people in those days; but organised Christianity, it seems, will disappear.

The second half of chapter 12 is taken up with conflict in

heaven. (See vv. 7–17). John sees Satan in heaven. Maybe, as Christians, we need to be reminded that Satan is depicted as having some limited access there. At the beginning of the Book of Job we find Satan going into God's court to request permission to deal tragedy to Job. Paul, as you know, is well aware that the real spiritual battles are fought beyond space and time, beyond flesh and blood, against the principalities and powers. (See Ephesians 6:12). The question I find myself asking, as John sees Satan hurled from heaven in the second half of chapter 12 of Revelation, is: How many times can he be thrown out? Have you ever asked yourself that? What event is John seeing here? Is it in John's future? Is it yet in our future? Is it John's present? —or his past? It seems to me – not necessarily taking this just from the text – that there can only be one banishing of Satan. Now the dragon in Scripture always refers to the enemy of God's people. You can see that in Psalm 74, Isaiah 27, Ezekiel 29. The only possible answer I can find is that, when Christ ascended the throne, when he came into the heavenly courts, both as Lion of Judah and as the Lamb who was slain, Satan's role in relation to heaven was forfeit. Satan, in Hebrew, means 'accuser', and Satan's role and his 'restricted access' in the heavens was linked with his ability to accuse God's people. Now that God's people are hid in the victory of Christ, wrapped in Christ's righteousness, sealed with the cross, it seems to me that there is no place in the heavenly courts for the accuser of men and women who have put their faith in God. True, there are several references in Scripture to Satan's fall, but I believe – and it is a personal view – that they all refer to the one event. Back in Isaiah, in the lament over the king of Babylon (Isaiah 14:12), Isaiah leaps ahead, as so often the prophets do, to something that is way ahead. I take the view that this is what Isaiah does, seeing the falling of Satan from heaven. Jesus himself saw, in the eye of his spirit, Satan fall from heaven, as the ministry entrusted to his disciples began to make inroads into Satan's kingdom. You remember the sending out of the seventy-two? They returned enthusing, and Jesus said, "I saw Satan fall like lightning from heaven." And I believe that, here, John is given a view of Satan's fall. Given all the horror that John has been predicting upon earth, given all the carnage of the demonic forces that are to be unleashed, John – and I think we – need a reminder that Satan is hurled from heaven. Again we notice, therefore, how Revelation displays a balance between awareness of the horror of so much that happens, and hopefulness. John has been foreseeing all this persecution coming upon the church; yet he now sees that Satan's powers are not infinite —rather, he is defeated. Notice too that – although his response is to attack us – Satan is defeated by the saints. (See 12:10–11). In verse 11, it is they who 'overcame him by the blood of the Lamb and by the word of their testimony; they did not love their lives so much as to shrink from death.' This word 'overcame', as we signalled at the beginning, is one of the key words of the whole book. Each time John, by the Spirit, writes a letter to the churches, he includes the phrase [To] '...him who overcomes... I will give ...' —and then there is a promise of reward. So there is an identification here of God's people with God in Christ. Jesus said, "But take heart! I have overcome the world" (John 16:33); and now we as God's followers, as Christ's disciples, putting our faith in him, are to work out that overcoming. Although the ultimate battle was really won at the cross, the way that you and I live our lives, the way that we speak, the way that we act, the way that we think, the way that we bear witness or do not bear witness to our faith, plays a part in the mopping-up operation. The outcome is no longer in doubt; but each individual combatant still needs to play a very careful part in making sure that the forces of the enemy are finally vanquished. We, the saints of God, can play our part in the remaining battles. We must note, as well, that – as often is the case with a human army – Satan's response to defeat is savage, albeit futile. Some of the worst atrocities of the last European war were perpetrated by the Nazis as they retreated, from Russia and from Western Europe. And Satan will be savage – if futile – where we give him the opportunity. But take comfort from the phrase (12:12) with which John ends here —that 'he knows that his time is short'. It seems to me that this is what Jesus was talking about on the Mount of Olives (Matthew 24:22): "...for the sake of the elect those days will be shortened."

The beast from the sea
13:1–10

Why should the beast come from the sea? You can search many commentaries in vain for an answer to this. We must recall the understanding of the sea in the Hebrew mind. It represented fear and chaos. Genesis 1 opens with the waters symbolising the chaos of our planet before God's creative power formed the world. It is fascinating that when we finally get to Revelation 21 and see the new creation, John witnesses that there was no longer any sea (i.e. fear and chaos).

As we read these words from chapter 13, we can also observe that there is a significant political dimension to them. We know this because of the power language employed: horns, crowns, authority. Note in 13:5–7 that while much power and authority was given to the beast, John is subtly reminding us that the beast is not an ultimate power. Of course, not all politics is beast-like. If we were reading Romans 13 instead of Revelation 13, we would see, in Paul's mind, a very different understanding of politics. In Romans 13 Paul depicts politics as God intended, working for the greater good of society, for the restraining of human sin and wickedness, and for the punishment of wrongdoers. But Paul himself was very well aware that things would not always be like that. In 2 Thessalonians 2 he talks of the man of lawlessness, who would one day exalt himself in God's holy place (possibly a reference to the abomination of desolation in Daniel 9:27 and Matthew 24:15). In Revelation 13 we find politics as Satan corrupts it. Elsewhere, John refers to this beast as the antichrist (recall that the word 'anti' means 'in place of') —so the beast is seeking to usurp the place of the rightful occupier of the position. Paul and John clearly anticipated that in the last days (i.e. from Christ's ascension to his coming again) there would be various personifications of anti-Christian tyranny —and this is the figure of the beast

127

in Revelation 13. Of course, the questions everybody wants answered are: Who is it? What is it? Where is it?

This chapter, and especially the image of the beast, could be regarded as a case study which clearly exhibits the methodology I have been using: **observing a cyclical model, whereby we understand that John is seeing in recapitulations and from different viewpoints the same events over and over again.** You see here the problem with a linear model: if you start reading the Book of Revelation and think that it starts on a certain date in human history and then just goes through —you have all sorts of unnecessary problems. The greatest difficulty is that we are pushed into the realm of speculation. So, for the mediaeval reformers, the beast must be the papacy; for John's early readers, the beast must be Rome; for Christians in our own day, it has been identified variously by others with communism or with other religious systems. It is all too easy to look elsewhere for the mark of the beast. People have associated it with Napoleon, with Hitler, and so on. The seven heads of the beast, we are told later in chapter 17, are seven hills —well, that was a code for Rome in the first century. The contemporary writers used to refer to the city of seven hills when they meant Rome. So surely Rome must be the beast. But wait a moment— the city of Bath, where I live, is built on seven hills, too...! If you were listening to a sermon series on Revelation fifteen years ago, in a Western church, you would almost certainly have been told that the beast was world communism. After all, we learn in Revelation 17 that the beast is scarlet! When the European Community was about to admit its tenth member state a few years ago, there were certain Christians who got excited to the point of frenzy: surely this must be the beast – ten heads; ten crowns! When they admitted the eleventh member, it all died down rather. But still the ideas persist. You can go on the internet and you will find 'exposures' of plots to divide the world into ten administrative zones. It seems to me that the sheer subjectivity of such speculation reveals its weakness. The cyclical model avoids these problems. The beast is all of them and none of them. Yes, there may well be a final outworking, a final personification, or manifestation of anti-Christian tyranny, at the End; but we can see the beast all around us. It is a symbol of what the world and God's people can expect as history goes on. Note the description of the beast in verse 2: a leopard, a lion, a bear, and yet it is a hideous beast. Daniel (in chapter 7) saw four beasts: a leopard, a lion, a bear and an ugly one; and he told us that they represented successive empires —the Babylonians, the Persians, the Greeks, the Romans. Here, you see, John has fused them all together. It looks like a leopard; but, hold on, it has got feet like a bear; it has a mouth like a lion. This seems to be John's way of representing the sum of human tyranny down the ages. To John and his early readers, yes, the beast would be identified as Rome, but it is always more than Rome. The beast is government in its demonic perversion; evil made incarnate within the structures of political life. It is the earthly outworking of the principalities and powers of Ephesians 6. When political power gets into evil hands, it is a bad day for the world and for God's people. We are reminded of Lord Acton's famous dictum (often misquoted), 'Power tends to corrupt and absolute power corrupts absolutely.'

Let us look now at three characteristics of the beast. Firstly, there is **invincibility**, as shown in the fatal wound. (13:3). John depicts the beast as having an uncanny way of coming back, when you think you have beaten him. The Christians of the first century breathed huge sighs of relief each time an emperor died, and then the next one would be even worse. Or think of the last century – the century of revolution – when people tried to shake free of their oppressors. Lord Halifax once wrote this: 'When people contend for their liberty, they seldom get anything by their victory, but new masters.' So we exchange a Tsar for a Lenin; we exchange a Kaiser for a Hitler; we exchange a last emperor for a Chairman Mao; we exchange the oppression of colonialism for the oppression of communism.

Secondly – and perhaps astonishingly (and we need to learn this as Christians) – the beast is **popular**. There is an enormous political mirage, in the Western political mindset, that democracy is a sure barrier against absolute power and tyranny. Lincoln famously said, 'You can't fool all the people all of the time' —well, he probably had not met the beast! People are perfectly capable of electing the beast to office. Consider Hitler. The irony of the modern political obsession with elections is that sometimes we simply legitimise the rule of tyrants. Lord Acton, after his comment about power, went on to make this controversial comment: 'Great men are nearly always bad men; and there is no worse heresy than that the office sanctifies the holder of it.' People admire might and power. Look at what they say about the beast in verse 4: "Who is like the beast? Who can make war against him?" People will happily vote for Satan if he makes them feel strong.

The third characteristic is **totalitarianism** (see verse 8). This is the defining character of the beast. Governments can be militarily strong without being evil. Governments can be popular without being demonic. Such governments are happy with the notion 'Fear God and honour the king' —but not the beast. His demand is for total worship, total obedience, total submission, and that is what gives him away. Essentially, there are two theories of government in our world. On the one hand there is the constitutional model, which says that the state exists to serve the members of society. Such societies have a constitution —whether a written one, as in France and America, or, as in Britain, one that has grown up over the years and relies upon precedent. Here there is an understanding that the state is accountable to some higher power, whether that be God, or the greater good; but the state is not ultimate. On the other hand, you have the totalitarian understanding of politics, whereby the will of the state overrides any other consideration. Those are the states in which servants are able to carry out atrocities without a moral flinch. We recall the Nuremberg trials ('we were simply obeying orders') —government as Satan corrupts. The beast represents totalitarian political rule. In the Old Testament, of course, that was Egypt. Pharaoh is the first beast. By comparison, Israel's king could not even make laws, but simply acted as custodian of what God had given. The beast is the deified state. Julius Caesar abolished the constitution of Rome; and then Domitian took the title *dominus et deus* (lord and god). And notice one of the marks of the beast (13:5) —blasphemy; and in verse 7, war against the saints. But the beast has never been confined to any one period of human history; the beast appears all over the place. It does not even have to use religious language; as long as it gets the obedience it wants, it is happy playing 'god'. People must worship. The beast requires the allegiance that is legitimately God's alone. You may be asking how it is that people fall for it. It is not by force, is it? It is by choice. Look at those old newsreel films of the crowds fawning on Hitler in the 1930s.

The beast from the earth (13:11–18)

The answer to how the beast does succeed lies in the second beast: the beast from the earth. Note in 13:12, he 'made the earth and its inhabitants worship the first beast'. The second beast is the state religion which bolsters the tyrannical regime. It is a religion that persuades people to yield allegiance. In the first century it would have been all the paraphernalia of the emperor-cult. What about today? Another of our great myths in the Western world is that we have separated state and religion, in the name of tolerance. But we have not done so at all. This fantasy allowed us comfortably to identify the beast with communism and other creeds and foreign nations, but never with anything in our midst. But of course we have not banished religion from politics at all. We have simply replaced the religion of God with a godless religion —call it humanism, or capitalism, or socialism. But we must make no mistake, modern political ideology in many forms is the proper successor to the emperor worship of Rome. It may not use religious language, but it serves a religious function. Capitalism – consumerism – delineates many of the values by which people behave, does it not? It helps them to understand the world in which they are set, and it gives them a world-view upon which everything else in life may be based. And there are 'false prophets' by which the twenty first century beast seeks to rule you and me, and we are not even aware of it.

Let us look at a key technique that this beast uses: a deceptive public image. We might say today, 'He is a good spin doctor' or, 'He's got good PR'; 'He looked like a lamb, but he spoke like a dragon.' A deceptive public image is so often created. Propaganda is another technique he uses —impressive displays of power. In a superstitious mediaeval age false miracles would do. Christians are not immune to such things even today, and we have to be discerning in these matters. But in a rationalistic age the miracles of science will do just as well, because the aim is to show that the beast can deliver the goods. Thirdly, there is the cult of personality. Every totalitarian regime needs a good face, a charismatic leader. The image is always set up; whether it be the statues that littered the Roman empire of old, or the wall hangings in Nazi Germany, or portraits of the Leader in some countries today. Of course, today, we have television, and this provides another way the image of the beast really can speak to us. What politician today can make it, without looking good on screen? Of course, there are always those who are stubborn; for those who will not be fooled and who will not bow the knee there is always good old-fashioned terror where necessary. (See v. 15.) Once failure to bend the knee to political orthodoxy has become an offence punishable by death, you know the beast is in power. And in verse 16 – probably the most disconcerting of all – the beast dominates the market. Do we only see the beast today in the obvious candidates —totalitarian regimes? Look at the power wielded by Western democracies. Do the political institutions of Europe have enough moral basis to handle the power that is being given to them? Do those in Britain and Europe, America and other places, who rush to centralise economic power, realise what a beast they might be unleashing if it was turned against the people? Do the vast corporations of capitalism, with their disregard for the environment, for indigenous peoples and for the people they employ, understand what a beast they may be nurturing? In

processing millions of human lives by numbers, are modern
governments furnishing the beast with the ability to make
his mark? I suggest the beast is not a remote figure. The
beast is growing under our feet, flexing his muscles within
the structures of political life and the institutions of which
you and I are so proud. Yes, the beast is, of course, to be
found in the obviously tyrannical states, but equally in
the dehumanising tyranny of big business politics, or the
paternalistic tyranny of 'Big Brother' socialism. In 1953
the Hoover Report in America said that, 'Although he may
not be aware of it, the Government in one form or another
accompanies the American citizen as an uninvited guest
almost everywhere he goes and in almost anything he does.'
You see, the cunning and subtlety of the false prophet is to
make you and me think that it is all the other people in the
world who are the victims of the beast.

So what, then, is our response to the beast? What is the
Christian's response to the beast? First, we must re-affirm
that the fundamental tenet of the Christian faith is 'Jesus
is Lord' —not just 'my Lord', but simply 'Lord'. And, if
people do not know that Jesus is Lord, it is my right and
duty, as a Christian, to tell them. Such a creed has political
consequences. So do not let anybody tell you that religion
and politics must be kept apart. No Christian can surrender
to a mere human institution, be it political, economic or any
other. The obedience we owe is owed to God alone. You
cannot serve two masters, Jesus taught. And that is why the
beast always persecutes the church. We seem to imagine
that if Christianity could only keep its nose out of politics,
we would all be safe. But every time Christians gather to
worship Jesus as Lord, we expose the beast as the illegitimate
usurper of the throne. And it seems to me that is the key to
understanding 666. You may know that Hebrew and Greek
letters have not just a literary value, but a numerical value
as well; and it was a pastime in the first century to work out
what your name meant in numbers. In Pompeii, when they
began to excavate, they found this graffiti: 'I love her whose
name is 545' – so romantic! Books have been written about

who is 666. One of the classic theories is that it is Nero —but that only works if you translate Nero into Hebrew and make a spelling mistake. Not really very convincing. I think the key is that perfection in this system would be represented as 777, and that Jesus' 'name' was 888 —and that seems to have been a secret code amongst early believers, to avoid persecution. You could talk about Jesus without actually saying Jesus (888). So, to me, 666 – and I am sorry if you are into all the hype – is absolutely nothing more than John blowing a literary raspberry to the beast. It is a comment on the beast's inferiority. John tells us as much in v. 18 —'It is man's number.' Jesus is 888; the beast is 666. Do not give him your worship —the beast is just a man, just a human thing, not a saviour or a lord.

But notice the implications of our worship and our belief. There is no such thing as private religion —and that can come as a shock to many members of my own denomination. Every Christian act of worship is a public declaration of God's sovereignty. To believe that, and to say it, is to denounce the beast wherever he appears. If you are a Christian, if your name is written in the Book of Life, if you are sealed —you cannot worship the beast. Notice in 13:8 that distinction is clearly made. Those who do not worship the beast are those who have Christ's name, who belong to the Lamb. So how do Christians protest? Not by taking up arms, but by taking up the cross (see verse 10). There are times when the only place a Christian can maintain integrity is in prison or on the scaffold. This is the power that Christianity represents —a power that can never be defeated, whereas the power of the beast is coercive, forcing people to do what they do not want to do. But the power of Christ is nailed to a cross; it oppresses nobody, it coerces nobody. The church makes its stand in suffering —not some terror campaign, but in simple witness. And whenever there is Christian witness – perhaps even martyrdom – it makes life hard for the beast. It is easy to understand why Rome persecuted the early Christians for treason. Communism, too, imprisoned Christians for fear that Christians would bring the whole edifice crashing down. 'Jesus is Lord' is a statement which exposes every impostor aspiring to the throne of God.

Revelation 14
The Lamb, 144,000, 6 angels and a couple of harvests

Again it seems that part of what John is doing is achieving balance. John relieves the horror of the chapters we have just been looking at by showing us, in contrast to those who bow to the beast, those who wear a different mark, the name of God. Notice that the mark of the beast is cryptic and confusing, whereas the name put upon Christians is clear. We have noticed what sealing does: it is God's way of declaring, 'These are mine, these are genuine and they may not be touched.' The number appears to be symbolic, pointing to – and we are told that these are the first groups – the magnificent number that will one day gather in glory. The remainder of the chapter is taken up with these angels. The third angel speaks of the terrible consequences of submitting to the beast. You can read of them in vv. 9ff. If anyone worships the beast, '...he, too, will drink of the wine of God's fury, which has been poured full strength into the cup of his wrath. He will be tormented with burning sulphur in the presence of the holy angels and of the Lamb.' And that word 'torment' is the same word used when the beast is thrown into the lake of fire, in Revelation 20:10. In other words, if you put your faith in the beast, you share the fate of the beast. It is a terrible opposite to the Christian hope of being hid in Christ, and sharing his wonderful inheritance.

The 4th, 5th and 6th angels seem to enact the harvests of the earth. Both the righteous and the wicked are harvested; and the chapter closes with another fairly horrific picture of wrath and judgment: grapes are gathered and are trodden in the winepress of God's fury, so that the blood flows deep and thick. Do we acknowledge in our hearts the strength of Scripture's teaching about the judgment that is coming for those who choose the beast? Yet, even here, the gospel is proclaimed. There is the link between wrath, blood and wine throughout Scripture. James and John asked for the best seats in heaven. Jesus replied, "Can you drink the cup I am going to drink?" (Matthew 20:22b.) The clever response of a knowledgeable Jew at that time would have been, 'Actually, no', because the 'cup' always means wrath and judgment. And it throws a poignant light upon Gethsemane. 'Gethsemane' literally means a winepress, or an oil press. It comes from a root word meaning crushing. In Gethsemane, and on the cross, your Saviour and my Saviour, was crushed, and his blood flowed for us, precisely to provide all humanity with a means of escape from the coming judgment. Right at the heart of God's judgment is the key to salvation. Even amid the many vivid images of the Book of Revelation, there stands the cross.

Let me just ask you this: What marks your life today? Is it the cross —the mark of Christ? Or do you bear the mark of someone else?

Heavenly Father, we praise you that in Christ we have salvation. Lord, we ask you to help us to be faithful in sharing the knowledge of your gift of salvation with others. We ask you, too, to keep us faithful to you, whatever may come our way. We pray that we may always be those who are sealed, always be those who are yours, always be those who bear your name. We ask it in Jesus' name. Amen.

9

MORE CHARACTERS
IN THE DRAMA
Revelation 17 – 18

We return now to 'characters in the drama' —and we meet two women towards the end of the Book of Revelation, who represent two cities. You could indeed say that Revelation draws to a close with a tale of two cities. In chapters 17 and 18 we meet Babylon, portrayed as a coarse and brazen prostitute; and in chapters 21 and 22 the New Jerusalem, the bride of Christ. The chapters that stand between the two (19 and 20) represent the great gulf that exists, separating the two cities.

Here, in Revelation 17 and 18, we have Babylon; but what does John mean us to understand by 'Babylon'? Let us have a closer look at her. One of the seven angels addresses John.

"Come, I will show you the punishment of the great prostitute, who sits on many waters. With her the kings of the earth committed adultery and the inhabitants of the earth were intoxicated with the wine of her adulteries."
Then the angel carried me away in the Spirit into a desert. There I saw a woman sitting on a scarlet beast

that was covered with blasphemous names and had seven heads and ten horns. The woman was dressed in purple and scarlet, and was glittering with gold, precious stones and pearls. She held a golden cup in her hand, filled with abominable things and the filth of her adulteries. This title was written on her forehead:

MYSTERY
BABYLON THE GREAT
THE MOTHER OF PROSTITUTES
AND OF THE ABOMINATIONS OF THE EARTH.

I saw that the woman was drunk with the blood of the saints, the blood of those who bore testimony to Jesus.

So what does Babylon signify? How can we decode the mystery that is written on her forehead? In the Scriptures, most cities are regarded with suspicion. Think of Sodom, think of Nineveh. Originally, they appear in association with the line of Lamech, and they are associated with production of weapons of mass destruction, such as they were in the ancient world. Cities concentrate people; therefore they concentrate sinners; therefore they concentrate sin. This seems to be the Bible's understanding. Anonymity leads to brazenness, to abandon. Wordsworth would later refer to this in Book One of his Prelude as he visited London in the early nineteenth century and saw what he called 'the strife of singularity', this anonymity born of city life that seems to give people license to behave in ways that they otherwise would not. Think of the writings of the social reformers in the nineteenth century and into the twentieth century —of children growing up in the great cities of Europe, who had no concept of animal life or of the sea or mountains, and so on. Cities are man-made, and of course self-made men and women worship their creation. Arrogance shows in architecture: buildings are testament to human egos. Sadly, many of our churches suffer from that, too. Such, you see, was the power of Babel, the first classic example of Scripture's understanding of the city; founded by Nimrod – himself a warrior and a hunter – on the belief that might is right, that strength will prevail. Babel's builders give themselves away (Genesis 11:4): "Come, let us build ourselves a city ... so that we may make a name for ourselves." Their arrogant desire could be said to have been the beginning of humanism. God's response to Babel was to give it many languages —resulting in confusion and lack of comprehension. That punishment was, of course, reversed in the miracle of Pentecost, where many languages were heard spoken and yet were understood by every listener. Later, Babylon became the capital of the greatest empire the world had yet known; and the same pride and arrogance can be seen in one of its greatest kings, Nebuchadnezzar. In Daniel 4:30, he is recorded as saying, "Is not this the great Babylon I have built as the royal residence, by my mighty power and for the glory of my majesty?" At the same time as condemning Babylon, the Scriptures offer us the contrast of another city, very different, not centred on the world's great trade routes, as Babylon was, not home to the world's greatest army, not a logical place to build a capital city; and yet which, today, is significant, as ancient Babylon lies in ruins. There is a city made special, because it was God's city, the place of his dwelling. Although Babylon appeared to triumph (Nebuchadnezzar, of course, was the king who razed Jerusalem), yet the Old Testament, as we read in Isaiah (and you can find similar prophecies in Jeremiah), was quite clear in predicting that Babylon would fall and Jerusalem would be restored. This begins to help us to understand what John means by Babylon.

We have been considering ways of interpreting Revelation and we saw that one of the most helpful ways is the cyclical approach —seeing John's visions as picture cycles of God's dealings with the earth, the way that history moves along. We have seen, too, that the problem with the linear model is that it leads us specifically to identify Babylon too closely, just as it did the beast, and other things. Think of Luther's railing against the Church of Rome, talking of the Babylonian captivity of the Church —you can still hear that in some churches today, virtually word for word, if you wish. And yes, of course, Rome did persecute believers at various stages in its history; but it does not do justice to John's picture of Babylon here. Part of the reason that so many Protestant interpreters have seen Babylon as Rome is because, in the Old Testament, when Israel – God's people – is faithless and breaks the covenant, she is described in terms of immorality, of adultery and prostitution. The trouble is, this does not fit the picture of the woman on the scarlet beast that John paints for us. She is not breaking a covenant because she has never had one. The two sins that are singled out as Babylon's sins are greed and pride. Think again of Jesus' words, in Luke 16:13, "You cannot serve God and Money." Babylon's sin is the prostitution of wealth and power, in the service of a culture which refuses to give glory to God. Of course, for John and the first Christians, Babylon was a symbol of Roman culture, and actually it is quite possible that the analogy with prostitution and immorality has less to do with Israel in the Old Testament than with the debauchery of contemporary Roman society. But John, again, in his text, gives us fairly strong hints that he is not intending this picture of Babylon to be limited to Rome, any more than the beast can be identified with just one individual or system. We saw that John, in presenting us the picture of the beast, drew on Daniel's vision of four separate beasts. As we look into the detail of this text, we see that that is exactly what John does with this picture of Babylon.

If you look carefully at the text of Revelation chapter 17, you will find references to at least four different cities in various Old Testament prophets —Tyre (vv. 1 & 4 —Isaiah 23:17; Ezekiel 28:13); Babylon itself (vv. 1 & 4 —Psalm 137:1; Jeremiah 51:7,13); Gaza (v. 15 —Jeremiah 47:2); and even unfaithful Jerusalem (16, 17 —Jeremiah 29:16; Ezekiel 16:37, 39). There is also, in verse 9, a direct reference to Rome, a city commonly referred to as 'the city on seven hills' among Roman writers such as Virgil and Cicero. So John is, I believe, using 'Babylon' as a generalised, all-encompassing symbol for the godless culture which characterises the world in which we live, the godless culture which surrounds the Christian church; and which – as history draws ever nearer to its close – will gain an ever-increasing intensity. Babylon represents a world which knows materialism without morality, pleasure without purity, wealth without wisdom, lust without love; a world that is both corrupt and corrupting. John's Babylon represents humanistic, godless society; a world in defiance of God.

So how is Babylon characterised? Firstly, there is vast international influence. You may have been struck by the reference in 17:1 —she 'sits on many waters'. What a peculiar thing to say. What does this mean? Well, the angel goes on to explain in verse 15. "The waters you saw, where the prostitute sits, are peoples, multitudes, nations and languages." Babylon does not rule the kings of the earth by military conquest, or by fear or domination. She permeates the fabric of human society, just as water permeates sand. We see in 17:2 that the nations form alliances with her voluntarily, that she infatuates societies. They are fascinated, magnetised, intoxicated. But the intoxication is occult, as we learn in 18:23, "...By your magic spell all the nations were led astray." So the first characteristic of Babylon is globalism —vast international influence.

The second characteristic, we learn in 17:4, is a horrifying level of moral corruption and decadence. There is a shamelessness about Babylon, a brazenness, an abandon. She is a city riddled with moral corruption. But perhaps the chief characteristic and the one that should alarm us today, more than any of the others, is that Babylon is a place of enormous materialistic affluence. There is a description of the woman in verse 4, 'dressed in purple and scarlet, and was glittering with gold, precious stones and pearls'. Then, if you look at 18:12–13, you will see the luxury goods with which Babylon fills her streets: '... gold, silver, precious stones and pearls; fine linen, purple, silk and scarlet cloth; every sort of citron wood, and articles of every kind made of ivory, costly wood, bronze, iron and marble; ... cinnamon and spice, of incense, myrrh and frankincense, of wine and olive oil, of fine flour and wheat; cattle and sheep; horses and carriages; and bodies and souls of men.' Babylon glitters.

As we said, when thinking of the beast, some Christians want to identify all that is anti-Christian in Revelation with other nations, or with communism, for example. So, they say, the woman riding the beast is that pervasive creed of Marxism. But until recently you could not imagine finding those luxury goods in Moscow's streets; nor would you have found much of that sort of thing in Beijing or Havana. It hardly fits, does it? This is not Marxism. Rather, Babylon is a global economy, based on luxury goods, a worldwide culture, where extravagance is admired and advertised. Well, we can buy these goods, wherever we look in our own cities: gold and silver, linen and cloth – there are the fashion houses; ivory and bronze – surely the auction houses of the big cities; cinnamon and spice —we think of luxury cosmetics. And 'bodies and souls of men' —what a chilling addition these words represent in John's list. In a Babylonian economy, everything is bought and sold, everything is for sale, everything has its price, even the bodies and souls of men and women. In a Roman world, of course, there was literally the slave market, to which you could go along to pick out your choice of slave. Well, surely we are more sophisticated, these days, we say —we got rid of slavery long ago. Yet men and women are still enslaved in the name of the 'god' called money. Slavery still exists, quite literally, in some territories of the world today. And there have been many accounts of young women being lured to European countries into lives of prostitution. But we could also think of those who are working on mind-numbing production lines, just to bring in what the family needs to live. Even the more affluent are not immune to some features of 'slavery', though outwardly they may appear to have more freedom of choice. Consider the young, rising executive, who has to leave home before the kids wake, and gets back long after they are asleep. He does not have time for family life, because his company 'owns' him. It owns him by the pressure that it knows it puts upon him; because if he refuses to toe the line, his job will go to another, and then the mortgage will fail —and so on and so on. A friend of mine, on leaving university, got a job with one of London's merchant banks. He was clearly very good at his job and received promotion after promotion, until, having been offered promotion to the highest levels of the board of management, he was called in to see the managing director and was told that one of the consequences of this next promotion would be divorce. None of the people working above him in the company had a marriage that had survived. Do we not still trade in the souls and bodies of men and women, at all sorts of levels? The people who get rich in Babylon are the businessmen, the merchants, the traders. It has been estimated that in a recent year the average remuneration of the head of an average US company was $10.6 million. That represented an increase on the previous year's pay of 37% —while the average blue collar worker was given a 2.7% increase. Babylon is a world where wealth alone determines how you are regarded.

Babylon is the epitome of the global market economy —capitalism in all its gaudy affluence and thinly-veiled cruelty. In 1993 the world's trade ministers signed what is known as the Uruguay Round Agreement, which slashed trade barriers by an average 40%. The effect on the poorer nations of the world has been catastrophic: smaller scale farmers cannot compete with huge, cheap imports. The European Union has for years had a policy of dumping foodstuffs at below the cost of production in developing countries. Whereas Jerusalem witnessed at its best to the rule of God among mankind, Babylon epitomises the selfish rule of mankind in defiance of God, a world in which money talks, money rules; a world of self-indulgent, covetous consumerism, in which all that matters is money.

John seems to me to be painting a picture a little too close to home for comfort. Notice, in 17:3, that Babylon rides the beast. We saw earlier that the beast is a picture, for John and for us, of demonic perversion of political rule —totalitarianism, wherever it is found, the sort of political rule which is intent on usurping God's rightful place. It is no surprise, then, that the godless pursuit of wealth should be associated with such a beast, but notice John's astonishing insight. Writing in the world in which he did, he foresaw a world in which economics would rule politics, where politicians would be bought and sold as commodities, when power would actually lie in the hands of the great men of trade of the world. One of the concerns with economic globalism is that it concentrates power and wealth in the hands of a handful of multi-national corporations. It is estimated that over 95% of the world's trade is in the hands of around 300 such corporations. And John tells us in 17:18: 'The woman you saw is the great city that rules over the kings of the earth.' Are you sitting uncomfortably? You should be. The picture of Babylon should disturb us, because we are buried in it, up to our necks and our wallets and our pay cheques.

But we must note two further things about Babylon: Babylon is anti-Christian, and Babylon is doomed. You see in 17:6, and again in 18:24, that Babylon flows with the blood of the saints. Babylon is a city of martyrs. There is no place for a holy people in a city devoted to corruption. For the moment, Babylon in the Western world might be content to buy the church's silence, to buy the church's complicity, or to ridicule us to the edges of society where the voice of the gospel is not heard. But if God should revive us, if the Holy Spirit should come upon us and change us into that radical, transforming people that we are called to be, well, Babylon will have no hesitation in baring its teeth. Babylon is a city that does not want a conscience. Babylon is an anti-Christian culture and Babylon is doomed. We saw a hint of that in 14:8, and we see it again through these chapters.

The fall of Babylon is examined in Revelation 18. We notice that John tells us several things about the fall of Babylon. Firstly, that it is dreadfully tragic. Look at 18:22–23,

> The music of harpists and musicians,
> flute players and trumpeters,

will never be heard in you again.
No workman of any trade
will ever be found in you again.
The sound of a millstone
will never be heard in you again.
The light of a lamp
will never shine in you again.
The voice of bridegroom and bride
will never be heard in you again.

It is so tragic. You see, Babylon is not a place of unmitigated evil: there is music ordained by God for his praise; craftsmanship; marriage and family life, all intended to be a blessing. Urbanised industrial consumer society is not unremittingly evil; and we would do well to recognise the artists and the poets and the craftsmen in our world, who – even if misguidedly – are striving to represent and respond to the creative mark upon them. But sin is so impregnated into our world that, when judgment comes, everything will be swept away.

If the fall of Babylon is tragic, it is also dramatic. Note the arrogance in 18:7–8,

'I sit as queen; I am not a widow,
and I will never mourn.'
Therefore, in one day her plagues will overtake her.

Arrogance is the hallmark of Babylon through the ages: Babel, Nebuchadnezzar and so on. And here it is the arrogance of economic complacency —'I'm alright....' And notice again in 18:23, 'Your merchants were the world's great men.' Here is another extraordinary insight from John, looking ahead to a world where it would no longer be the politicians or the generals who would be the world's great men; the merchants are the kingmakers in Babylon. We should not then fear so much, perhaps, the power of nuclear war, but rather the power of the dollar, the euro, the yen or sterling, the traded derivatives and 'futures'. Big business calls all today's tunes. The beast's final show will be a global business empire, in which financiers and big business chiefs are our kingmakers. And yet, says John, this seemingly invincible global system will crash; Babylon's arrogant complacency will suddenly be totally and unexpectedly shattered. Note the strength of the poetic language: '...in one day her plagues will overtake her...In one hour your doom has come ... In one hour such great wealth has been brought to ruin.' It will not be a gradual recession, then, for Babylon, but a dramatic collapse. Many crises have shown us just how fragile the world's economic systems are. What John foresees here is so feasible today.

The fall of Babylon is ironic, for it is the beast on which Babylon rides which will destroy her. Babylon, you see, achieves her dominant position in close collaboration with the beast and the kings of the earth. Political will yields to the power of money. The kings are mesmerised, by Babylon's glamour, into worshipping her; and Babylon rides them all. Economics dominates politics. But the seeds of Babylon's destruction lie within her. The route she took to power is the means by which she will fall. Political turmoil will toss Babylon from the back of the beast. However affluent Babylon seems, she cannot withstand the turmoil of politics.

Note the response of heaven. The fall of Babylon is welcomed by heaven. We peep over the garden wall into Revelation 19:1–6 and we see the original Hallelujah Chorus! Although the fall of Babylon is mourned by the kings of the earth, the merchants and the traders, heaven rejoices. How many people in our world would still sing, or listen to, the Hallelujah Chorus, if they knew that it was written in praise of the collapse of the unrestrained capitalist system; that what they were singing about was heaven's chorus of joy over banks falling and stock markets crashing? We are used to the idea that heaven rejoices at repentance. But are we so comfortable with the idea that heaven rejoices at judgment? Heaven feels no sympathy for evil. We might get ever so embarrassed about the concept of hell, but heaven displays no such embarrassment. Heaven sees evil for what it is. It sees that evil has scarred God's creation; it sees the lives ruined, the endless litany of tragic lament that rises from the face of the earth; the abused children, the shattered hopes, the cruelty, the injustice. Heaven sees evil for what it is: hideous in its ugliness, outrageous in its insolence, and deserving of judgment. We read the words, 'God so loved the world', and we tend to think, 'Oh well, the world can't be such a bad place then, if God loved it.' As if, to be the object of God's love, the earth must also be the object of his admiration. The Bible teaches us that God loves, in order that some might escape the coming judgment. The love of God is not a compliment paid for the earth's goodness. It is an expression of his grace, which is at once undeserved and unprovoked. Eternity will shed no tears at the fall of Babylon. There will be no nostalgia in heaven for planet earth when it falls. For the one who now appears, as we peep over the wall into Revelation 19, is as beautiful and pure as Babylon is ugly and corrupt. Who could regret the exchange?

So how does the Christian respond to Babylon? The author of Hebrews 11 urges us not to settle —to come out of Babylon, as we are told in Revelation 18:4,

> "Come out of her, my people,
> so that you will not share in her sins...."

We come out of Babylon by refusing to make this world our home, by refusing to be ensnared in a culture whose values are humanism and materialism, whose characteristics are greed and pride, where people are valued solely according to their economic means. I want to suggest a practical way you can begin the process of coming out of Babylon. Sort out your attitude to money. Who is your God? You might want to commit yourself to a period of prayer and fasting, as you work on this area. If you have never fasted before, talk to somebody who has done it, and get proper advice on the way to go about it. You might decide to give up some things for a while; be led by the Spirit in the matter of abstinence or moderation in various areas of life. Take the time to pray, time that you would otherwise take 'living in Babylon' in your luxuries and your comforts. The call of God's Spirit to come out of Babylon is a call to a journey. We are the *real* travellers of God's 'new age' —in the sense that we are the pilgrim people God has called to be his own. Once we begin to settle, we set down our roots in Babylon. Let us heed Jeremiah's warning. Leave the spiritual 'Babylon', run for your life from her deceptive principles; do not be destroyed because of her sin. It is time for the Lord's vengeance.

Finally, think of two roads in the New Testament: the road to Damascus along which Paul journeyed; and the road to Emmaus, along which those disillusioned disciples walked. The astonishing thing about both roads is that they are both actually the road to Jerusalem —it is just that Paul and the disciples were going the wrong way. But which way are you travelling? To Jerusalem? Or to Babylon?

Holy Spirit, guide me constantly, so that I may discern the right path, and keep to it, in Jesus' name. Amen.

10

A NEW BEGINNING
Revelation 19 – 22

When John begins to unfold the very final things which will occupy the last pages of human history, he points us to a a rider on a white horse, whose name is Faithful and True. (19:11) Hearing that name 'Faithful and True' is an amazing thing for us, in the cynical, world-weary, disillusioned age in which we live. That name reminds us to keep our eyes on Christ, who alone embodies and exemplifies those virtues. If you have 'learnt' the hard way that trust is a dangerous pathway in life, look to Christ, because the rider on the white horse is faithful and true. There is something mysterious about the rider. We read that he has a name written on him that no one knows but himself (v. 12). Here, John seems to be teaching us that no human mind can fully fathom the nature of God. It is what the fathers of the Eastern Church call the 'unknowability' of God; and there is this paradox in Scripture —there is a wonderful intimacy which Christians can enjoy with God, and yet, at another level, there is a great unknowability there as well. The rider may be slightly mysterious, but he is not anonymous, because in 19:13 we read that his name is the Word of God —so it is quite clear that this is Jesus. And at last, now, John unveils the

149

appearance which has been there in the background of the Book of Revelation since the 7th verse of the first chapter, where John wrote:

> Look, he is coming with the clouds,
> and every eye will see him....

Ever since that verse we have been wanting to know this: when is the appearing going to happen, when is it going to be revealed, when are we going to see him? All the way through, there have been hints. The curtain has been pulled aside, and then dropped again. But now we see the only reliable leader, the one who, above all others, is faithful and true. We might possibly imagine, in the human realm, a politician who is faithful and true, but would they ever get elected? Yet this faithful and true leader is not weak. He has power to achieve his purposes. 'Out of his mouth comes a sharp sword with which to strike down the nations. "He will rule them with an iron sceptre."' (19:15). So, at last, there is going to be a leader who is morally upright, full of integrity, the model of faithfulness, the very essence of truth, and yet who will actually be able to accomplish the best hopes and dreams of the human heart. The nature of the rider on the white horse begins to be revealed, and John takes his stand – very unpopularly today – quite clearly, alongside all the other writers of Scripture, showing us that when Christ returns he will engage upon a just and holy war.

Now, of course, many people, within and outside the church, complain about this image. Jesus, gentle, meek and mild – 'no crying he makes' —we have such a sloppy view of Jesus. Most people cannot get near him for the cotton wool. It is just as hard for the human mind to understand the power and the awesomeness of wickedness and evil, despite the many horrors in the pages of history and in the modern world. The capacity of most people to apprehend either perfect goodness or terrible evil is extremely limited. So they fail to see why the two are inevitably at war. One of the key messages of the whole of the New Testament, including

Revelation, is that the world really is in a state of war. God may have created the world, but the creatures of God have rebelled. They have staged a coup. And the coup has temporarily had a measure of success. Many have joined Satan's ranks; many have taken their place with the rebels. Some are in the pay of the enemy. Most just keep their heads down, and collaborate for a quiet life. This world is enemy-occupied territory; that is the picture we gain not only from John, but from the New Testament as a whole.

The whole of the Bible – and supremely the Book of Revelation – is the story of the king's counter-attack. When we realise the authority and power of Christ, we recognise that God could have invaded this world and forced submission on his rebellious subjects, at any point. But he chose not to. Instead he chose a two-phase attack. The first, in fact, was the Incarnation – the babe of Bethlehem. God became man. To extend the military metaphor, you might say that Christ came unarmed, like a civilian. His purpose was threefold:

1. To engage the enemy in single mortal combat, and to deal him a deadly blow.

2. To release prisoners – to set men and women free from the hold of the enemy – and to establish in their ranks a resistance. You and I are part of the resistance movement for planet earth.

3. To prepare for the day when the kingdom, that Christ secretly sowed behind enemy lines, would be reoccupied in force.

As John writes, phase one is complete. All of that has been achieved. Now John paints for us pictures of phase two of the reoccupation: the king returns, heaven's doors open and the king rides out. No longer does he appear alone —notice the countless angels. No longer is he in disguise —note the many crowns. No longer is he unarmed —observe the sword. It is the same Jesus, just a different mission. When Jesus walked the earth, he came to proclaim the year of the Lord's favour. It was the season of the gospel, the time for repentance, the moment for redemption. Now the rider on the white horse brings not the day of favour, but the day of vengeance.

When Jesus returns, it is as a conquering king. Even his eyes will be daunting for those who look into them, because they will blaze with fire. What John unfolds to us in Revelation 19 is a systematic conquest of every rebellious force that he has introduced in the pages of the book. And notice how the characters are defeated in the reverse order from that in which they appeared. The beast who we discovered represents godless politics and the false prophet, which represents godless religion, are defeated in 19:20. In 20:10, Satan himself, the arch-enemy, is defeated. Then, in what is surely one of the most terrifying pictures in the whole of Scripture, from 20:11–15, we are shown the picture of judgment, when every human being will stand before the white throne of God. The book will be opened, and your life and my life, your words and my words, your deeds and my deeds, your thoughts and my thoughts, will be displayed; and the judgment will be enacted. John is quite clear here: whatever we think, however much we dislike it, he is absolutely adamant both that this world is at war and that Jesus will win, and that all those who persist in their course of rebellion will be judged and punished. That is not a popular thing to say today, but no preacher who is faithful to the Scriptures can say otherwise.

It is only after Revelation 19 and 20 that we can begin to read Revelation 21 and 22. It is only on the basis of a cosmos purged of evil that we can see the new created order. So that is what we see in Revelation 21 and 22 —the new city, Jerusalem, coming down out of heaven from God, prepared as a bride, beautifully dressed for her husband. Are you a little surprised to find that John's image of eternity is a city? Perhaps it is an unexpected symbol of your final destination. Think of the cities you know. Do they remind you of heaven? Most of us are not waiting and hoping for a city, but that is what John reveals —a holy city. And what does a city mean? It means people living together; it means organised social living, and that is precisely what John intends us to take from this. Most Christians still have too ethereal and insubstantial an idea about the afterlife, coloured by certain Greek views that can be traced back to the influence of the classical tradition of Plato and other philosophers. There is a Western tradition of metaphysical dualism in which non-physical reality is esteemed as superior to the messy material reality of the physical created order. That sort of dualism can very quickly lead us astray. It was precisely into this physical, material world that God came in the Incarnation. So the picture of the city, with its associations that are human, social, relational, and unashamed of the material created order, is far richer in meaning than we might at first think. As an image, it saves us from thinking of some insubstantial ghostly world of forms. The holy city is real! And the real dividing line is not where the Greek philosophers might have set it but between Creator and his creation. The heavens, with the angels and other heavenly beings who do the will of God and worship him, are part of the created order.

We will see wars and rumours of war. We will see natural disasters, persecution of the church, proclamation of the gospel. We will see beasts and false prophets and anti-Christs. And, as the days of human history draw to their end, we will see, in the last days, an intensification of the signs. We will see – I believe – the beast, whether an individual or an institution, the tribulation, cosmic distress and so on. And then there will be Christ's return, described in Matthew 24 and in Revelation 19. The dead in Christ will rise. Those living in the earth will be raptured. We will all receive our new bodies. Then follows the millennium and the *second resurrection*, and then the judgment and destruction of the present cosmos. Then we are ushered into the new heavens and the new earth. The chart at Appendix 1 sets out how all this fits together in Revelation, as a diagram.

One of the confusions which arises is a misunderstanding of what we call the intermediate state. In other words, what happens to you when you die. The Bible really has two words for that: Hades (the Hebrew word) and Sheol (the

Greek equivalent). They mean all manner of things in the Scriptures: from very simple things like just the grave, but also the place where those who die go. There is quite clearly a distinction in Scripture between those who die and go to be in what Jesus called paradise (as he said to the thief on the cross), and those who do not, who go to a place of darkness and wailing and gnashing of teeth. Then there will be the future creation: new heavens, new earth, and hell.

The Greek influence has made us think that a shadowy afterlife existence is permanent. But the Bible does not teach that. Paul describes the state of being away from the body as being imperfect. He talks in Romans 8 of a straining for our new bodies. Remember that we are looking for a city. It will be a marvellous, beautiful, solid city. Re-read 21:11 to 22:5 —'It shone with the glory of God, and its brilliance was like that of a very precious jewel ... It had a great, high wall with twelve gates....' —It is beautiful. And through the centre of the city flows a river, and by the river grows the tree, whose leaves are perpetually in bloom, '...and the leaves of the tree are for the healing of the nations.' What John is describing is a garden city. All the language and pictures he uses are symbols of perfection – the measurements, the imagery – to communicate to us what is difficult for our limited imaginations to grasp. But one thing we can say is that our eternal destiny is not some ethereal, insubstantial existence. It is not even a renewed Eden. It is not a garden, but a garden city. Note also where it is: 'I saw the Holy City, the new Jerusalem, coming down out of heaven from God...' (21:2). You see, there is still an up and down in the new order of things. There is still a heaven and there is still an earth. And Jerusalem descends from heaven —God's gift to his people. What did Jesus say of the meek? They will inherit the third cloud on the right, beyond Mars? No —they will inherit the earth.

Revelation 21 and 22 are the final hope, the final destiny of the company of God's people. In 22:5 we read that this state is for ever and ever. So the Christian hope is material, it is social and it is perfect. Peter writes, '...we are looking forward to a new heaven and a new earth, the home of righteousness' (2 Peter 3:13). We notice in 21:24 that cultural diversity will continue. There will still be nations, they will still be governed by kings. But unlike the kings of the earth who wage war against one another, they will be occupied in bringing their splendour into the gates of God's city. In 22:2 we read that the old divisions and hatreds of human existence will disappear, because there will be healing for the nations. It seems to me that one of the great implications – often unnoticed in John's writing – is that in heaven, in the new earth, in eternity, there is progress, there is development.

I believe there will also be time, maybe not quite as we see it – the tick-tock drudgery, the inexorable approach of the grave – but certainly movement. There is progression in eternity. There is a glorious cosmopolitan harmony awaiting us in the city of God. And there are practical implications as we await this new order. The first relates to the way we see our world and the social problems in our world. It should inspire our social concern and our social action for areas of privation in our society. John describes the state for which we are to hope as a city. All those Old Testament images of Jerusalem, the city of peace, will be brought to the most glorious fulfilment —a city where righteousness dwells. Has there ever been a city where righteousness dwells? No, there has not. But there will be: a city where you and I will live in perfect harmony with creation. A city in which labour will bring joy and fulfilment. But we are realistic enough to know that it is no human utopia. Neither Marxism nor any other humanly devised political system can achieve this. People have always longed for a 'new world', which is why, when they landed in America, that is what they called it. A city name like 'Philadelphia' – brotherly love – shows the hopes that they had. Yet Philadelphia today no doubt shares the crime and social problems of other cities in the world. The only thing man ever builds is Babylon. Think of that awful hymn by Blake: 'And did those feet in ancient times walk upon England's...' Well, no, frankly! They did not. And we are not going to build new Jerusalem on planet earth. New

Jerusalem is not a continuation of human history. New Jerusalem is not the final flowering of human achievement. It actually represents a radical discontinuity. New Jerusalem comes down from heaven —God's new creation, given to us. It stands on the other side of the line which the return of Christ will draw across the page of human history. But there is nothing ethereal about it. Glory is solid. It should inspire our social concern and our social action because, as a church and as Christians, we ought to be setting up signposts all over the planet to the new Jerusalem. People ought to look to what we do as a church and see glimpses of the new order, here and now.

Secondly, this vision should strengthen our commitment to the church. Notice, in 21:2, that the new Jerusalem is a symbol of God's people, the church. It is so easy to knock the church and make jokes about it. We are all too aware of the failings of its many denominational institutions. Some feel that they can be more Christian by not going to church. But every Christian, by definition, is in the church, the body of Christ. God's new order is God's people in social form. To be a Christian now is to be part of an entirely new social order, ahead of time. Augustine said there is no salvation outside the church; and, although those words have been abused over the centuries, there is still truth in them. Get stuck into the church, because one day, John's vision shows us, it is going to be the bride of Christ.

This local community of the church, despite all its faults, prepares us for the new order that is to come. You are going to have to get on with the person sitting next to you in church, in eternity. Would it not be a good idea to get some practice in now? Whatever your experience of church, you are nearer heaven when you are worshipping with other believers than when you are in isolation at home. Church may seem dull and unexciting now, but on its wedding day, you will not be embarrassed to belong!

John gives some beautiful images of what the new world order is going to be like. Those who live in the new world will enjoy a level and a dimension of joy that is completely beyond what we can imagine: '...for the old order of things has passed away' (21:4). When sin entered the world it corrupted the whole environment. It brought in sickness and decay and disease and death, natural disasters, enmity, hatred, division, quarrelling —and it separated us from God. John's picture language in chapters 21 and 22 of Revelation paints out everything which mars human existence. We learn in 21:1 that there will no longer be any sea. Well, that may come as a shock if you enjoy swimming off the coast of Cornwall or the Mediterranean. But remember that for the Jews, the sea was the symbol of chaos and of evil. Think of how the whole thing started, in Genesis 1. Why was there chaos? —because the planet was covered in water. What was the punishment that God visited upon the earth in the days of Noah? Flooding. How did the people of Israel escape? Through the Red Sea. When did the disciples really become afraid? Out on Galilee. For the Jewish mind, the sea remains a symbol of all that is chaotic. Where did the beast emerge from in Revelation 13? From the sea. John is telling us here that there will be no place for chaos and evil in the new world order. But if you like swimming, there is still the river of the water of life. Even I could probably swim really fast in the river of the water of life.

John also tells us that there will be no more suffering (21:4). Tears will be wiped away. That is one of the most beautiful images in Scripture. God himself is going to wipe the tears from your eyes. Tears are such an eloquent language. You turn on the television and you see refugees, or people whose homes have been destroyed in earthquakes. You cannot understand a word they say, but their tears tell you what is in their hearts. All human joy and every human achievement sooner or later is overshadowed by the approach of death. Some Christians seem blind to the reality of life. They say, 'Christians shouldn't cry. Whatever we are going through, as long as we just praise God, everything's alright.' They want us to behave as if heaven is already here, as if the new Jerusalem has already descended. It is a great error. Christians can and do weep, as Jesus did. We still have tears because there is still pain. We weep because there is still death. But Christians should be content above all people, because we know that one day tears will end. Pain still hurts. Grief still savages our emotions. Old age still frustrates us. Sickness still disheartens us. But Christians know that it is not to be forever. Christians should be the most contented of people, because they have hope. And what is the one thing that is lacking above all things in our world today? It is hope. In the last days of planet earth, whenever those days come, people will need the hope we Christians have.

In 21:6, we learn that there will be no more dissatisfaction. Everything that disappoints you today, everything that stands as a weight and a blight on your memory, everything that frustrates and exasperates —it is all going to go. Then, in 21:9, John introduces a beautiful image. One of the seven angels, who had the seven bowls full of the seven last plagues, does something like the work of a tour guide in the new order: "Come, I will show you the bride, the wife of the Lamb", he says to John. Clearly, the days of wrath are at an end.

In 22:5, we are told there is going to be no more night. Night is always a symbol of evil and darkness. Then, supremely, in 22:3, 'No longer will there be any curse.' That was the ultimate penalty that Adam and Eve paid for rebellion —they were placed under a curse. Ever since then, men and women have struggled under the weight of the curse, the penalty of sin. Yet we know that in Christ on the cross the penalty has been paid. Paul writes to the Galatians that the penalty for sin has been paid, because Christ became a curse for us. The day is coming when God's people will be removed from the very presence of the curse. In 21:25, John shows us there will no longer be any threat to peace. How amazing for John to conceive, in his ancient day, a city where the gates never shut. In John's world, every city shut its gates as night approached. Never need that happen in this city.

Notice the exquisite intimacy we will enjoy with God. In 21:7, see the image of parenthood. Whether or not you have a positive memory of your human father, I do know, from working with sufferers of child abuse, that they spend a long time dreaming of and imagining what a father could be. Take your best concept of 'father', multiply it thousands and thousands of times, and you might begin to get a glimpse of what God is talking about here. Recall that beautiful time in the garden of Eden, when God himself walked with Adam and Eve in the cool of the day? Now God makes his dwelling with his people and brings them very close to himself in that perfect family relationship.

Consider for a moment the image of matrimony (21:9) — people get concerned about this. Jesus taught that in heaven, in eternity, there will be no marriage. (See Matthew 22:30.) I have had people say to me, 'Well, if there's no marriage, I don't want to go.' But they are missing the point. What the vision of John is showing us is that the intimacy and the harmony with all God's people in heaven is going to outshine even the deepest intimacy that humans can know here. In this life we feel that we can only draw close maybe to one person for life and have that intimacy and that tender exquisite joy; yet in the eternal city all citizens will live in that harmony. And we will see his face (22:3–4). Was that not the quest of the Old Testament? Was that not the great privilege granted to Moses, that he saw God face to face, as a friend? And one day that privilege is going to be yours and mine. And it is not going to be just a temporary thing. We will bask in the presence of God, as we bask in the light on a tropical beach —all the time. (See 21:5) "I am making everything new."

The very last chapter of the Bible is a new beginning, and all the potential is there again: the potential of discovery, the potential of wonder, of enterprise, of creativity, of culture, of human fulfilment and of joy —everything that stood at the fingertips of Adam and Eve in the garden is once again possible in the garden city, completely unhindered by the limitations of sin or selfishness or physical decay. Take the deepest joy you have ever known, remember the greatest fulfilment that has marked your life to date, magnify it a million times, and you begin to glimpse what God has in store for those who love him. No wonder the last words John ever wrote were, 'Amen. Come, Lord Jesus. The grace of the Lord Jesus be with God's people. Amen.'

Make this prayer your own: *Amen. Come, Lord Jesus.*

PART FOUR

Remaining Questions

11

THE RAPTURE DEBATE

For the Lord himself will come down from heaven, with
a loud command, with the voice of the archangel and
with the trumpet call of God, and the dead in Christ will
rise first. After that, we who are still alive and are left
will be caught up together with them in the clouds to
meet the Lord in the air. And so we will be with the Lord
for ever. Therefore encourage each other with these
words. Now, brothers, about times and dates we do not
need to write to you, for you know very well that the day
of the Lord will come like a thief in the night. While people
are saying, "Peace and safety", destruction will come on
them suddenly, as labour pains on a pregnant woman, and
they will not escape.

But you, brothers, are not in darkness so that this day
should surprise you like a thief.

1 Thessalonians 4:16–5:4

Historically, there have been two views in the church
as to what happens to Christians when they die. One
understanding has at its heart a particular interpretation
of Paul's words about falling 'asleep' in Christ. That could

suggest that the deceased person passes into a temporary condition of unconsciousness. Then, when you awake at the general resurrection (see John 11), time will have passed you by, as it were. The other reading of Scripture, which is one shared by many theologians in the reformed tradition, and to which I subscribe, is that when a Christian believer dies, he or she goes straight into the presence of God. If it were not so, it would be hard to make sense of those wonderful words of Jesus to the penitent thief crucified alongside him: "Today, you will be with me in paradise." If this were not the case, it would be extremely hard to comprehend the pictures we have received through John's revelations of the saints together in glory, seeing the Father.

I sometimes imagine that, for the Christian, the process and experience of death might be a little like that of being born. We know that an unborn infant is very aware of his surroundings. He can see, hear and taste. Yet what a confined space the womb actually is. We have no way of communicating to him the size and beauty of the world he is about to enter. Leaving the womb is a traumatic experience —it is, after all, the only place he has known, a place of security, familiarity and warmth. Birth literally delivers him into a world of such immensity compared with the womb, a world whose sights, sounds, colours, experiences, wonder, are so much greater than anything experienced in the womb, that memories of that nine-month existence soon fade. Might not death be somewhat similar for the believer? It is a traumatic experience —this world is, after all, the only place we have known, a place of security, familiarity and warmth. But if we take the Scriptures seriously, death literally delivers us into a new life of such immense potential that this life will seem as constraining as the womb. We will emerge into a new life whose sights, sounds, colours, experiences, wonder, are so much greater than anything we can presently imagine —to behold the very glory of God, no longer through a glass, dimly, but face to face; to hear God's voice, welcoming a good and faithful servant. If you have placed your faith in Christ, this is the experience which awaits you when you die. And yet we must remember that heaven, thus conceived as the paradise the faithful enter upon death, glorious and beautiful as it is, is not our final home. Heaven is in fact a waiting room, where we await 'that day' (the phrase the Bible uses to talk of the day of Christ's return). On that day, those who have died in the faith of Christ, and those of his followers who have the privilege of being alive on earth at the time of his return, will be resurrected, in glorious new bodies, ready for the inauguration of the new creation, which is our eternal home. Then we will not only see and hear God, but also feel God's touch wiping away life's tears of sorrow and disappointment. So Paul can write—

...we will all be changed —in a flash, in the twinkling of an eye, at the last trumpet....

1 Corinthians 15:51b – 52a

And all the faithful in Christ – living and departed – will assemble in the clouds, as we read in 1 Thessalonians 4. Now it sounds fantastic. It probably sounds more fantastic because the church has not preached it properly, as it should have done. It is no more so than a sea standing end to end, that a million people may walk through. It is no more so than the presence of God filling a temple made by hands. It is no more so than a body which had been dead for three days being resurrected by the very power of God. As a believer you are hidden in Christ, saved by Christ. And one day you will share the most amazing event ever: the rapture, when believers will be gathered together, as taught in 1 Thessalonians.

The expression 'rapture' is linked with all that the New Testament means concerning mortality being changed to immortality; the perishable into the imperishable. Christians have taken various positions on these matters, and the position adopted on the rapture is pivotal for one's understanding of the End times as a whole.

The most popular view amongst evangelical Christians in America and throughout the world is, I believe, fundamentally wrong, though nothing that we say about these areas of interpretation should in any way impair fellowship with Christians who hold other views. Those with whom I may disagree on a point of interpretation are still my brothers and sisters in Christ: I still want to pray with them and for them, to worship with them, to welcome them; and I hope they would feel able to extend the same courtesy to me. There is nothing in what I am saying here that is meant to diminish other Christians. But I do believe that church leaders have a responsibility before God, as they feel the Spirit leading, to point out where they think there is serious error in the body of Christ.

So what is the rapture? It is described clearly in 1 Thessalonians, as we saw in the passage at the head of this chapter. That is the clearest teaching on the rapture, and Paul lays it out exactly: those who die in Christ will come to life in the same way that Christ was resurrected. As Bible believing Christians we do not believe in reincarnation, we believe in resurrection. The body in which you are raised to life will be much, much better than the one you have now. And those who are privileged to be believers upon the earth at that day will be caught up to meet those who have already died, in the air. What a wonderful prospect. It is amazing. In the Greek original, the word used for rapture is, literally, 'to be snatched up', 'to be caught up'; and it is very similar in its double meaning to the English word 'transport', which can mean being physically moved from one place to another, or a 'transport of delight'. Recall the setting of Psalm 23 that reads: 'What transport of delight from Thy pure chalice floweth.' Now the great point at issue is when the rapture will happen. Essentially, the disagreement is whether it happens before the great tribulation or after it. It is significant that the key 1 Thessalonians passage which everybody acknowledges as the major teaching on the rapture is not only silent about that point, it does not even display any awareness that there is a question to be answered —and that apparent 'omission', here as elsewhere, is significant. Paul, writing to the Thessalonians, did not consider it necessary to spell out when this would be —and I consider that his silence speaks volumes. So then the secret rapture theory, which is a view that I will explain, is the view you will find in the majority of popular contemporary books on the end of the world. Most famously, at the moment, the series of novels 'Left Behind', begins with the secret rapture happening. It essentially divides the return of Christ – and this is one of the great problems with the theory – into a second and a third coming. The second coming (given that the first coming was Bethlehem) is invisible to the world, a private event. It is a fleeting visit by Christ for one purpose alone: to remove the faithful living on earth to be with him before the great tribulation kicks in. There is then a gap between that private return of Christ for the saints (normally the gap is seven years, because that is what is understood as the great tribulation from Daniel —Satan's little season), and when Jesus comes a third time *with* the saints. So Christ returns firstly invisibly, without warning – and that is a key facet of the theory – to gather the elect. It could happen at any moment. The novels that go into this envisage spectacular results from this secret rapture. You will have airliners crashing because their Christian pilots are removed. Operating theatres will suddenly be left with no surgeons; cars will crash because the drivers have gone. Then the third coming corresponds to classic Christian expectation, as Christ comes visibly on the clouds. Thus, Christ comes firstly *for* and then secondly *with* the saints. And this position is known technically as the pre-tribulation position, because it claims that the rapture will occur before the tribulation comes. Of course it is a very comforting idea. The elect will be snatched out of harm's way. There is nothing to worry about. The great tribulation that is coming on the earth will not have any impact on us.

The older view – and I believe the correct one, as I am going to try to explain – is known as post-tribulation: that actually the rapture occurs simultaneously with Christ's one and only return at the end of the great tribulation.

There is, more recently, a third view known as mid-tribulation. This is really only a variation on pre-tribulation, so, in essence, they are one and the same. So let us look at the origins of this novel doctrine. It may be illuminating to discover that it involves a Scotsman, an Englishman and an Irishman! It is hugely significant that there is no trace of this view anywhere in the work of any Christian thinker, anywhere in the entire history of the church, before 1830. Standing as we do at the beginning of the twenty first century, we have re-discovered some things that were taught by the early church. But I do not believe that the body of Christian truth today contains anything that was not known way back then. So I think this is significant: before 1830 this idea was just not there. It emerged in the teaching of the Scotsman, Edward Irvine. He left a church in Scotland to found the Catholic Apostolic Church in Albury, near Guildford in Surrey. He passed on his teaching to Dr Henry Drummond, who owned the Albury estate, and they held seminars to propound this new theory, which were attended by John Nelson Darby, the Irishman, who was actually an Anglican curate in Dublin! Now Darby went off to the USA and, among other things, he was instrumental in founding the 'Brethren' denomination, and when he went to the United States he persuaded Dr Scofield of his views. Of course Scofield produced the Scofield Bible, and the rest, as they say, is history. So that is really the origin of it. It is now taught in theological colleges across America. Now the secret rapture may sound wonderful – of course, it would be lovely to believe we are going to be snatched out of harm's way before all hell is let loose – but the trouble is that the secret rapture comes with a package; and the package, now greatly disavowed by many Christians, is dispensationalism. Again it was a creation of John Nelson Darby, who read in the Authorised Version, 2 Timothy 2:15, that the steward of God 'rightly divides' the word of God. Actually, the NIV better translates it as 'correctly handles' the word of God. But on that basis Darby decided it was up to him to divide Scripture and earth history into seven eras: what he called 'dispensations'. Well, that is nothing new. Christians have been doing that down the ages: there was the period of Genesis 1–11, the pre-history part; then you have the patriarchs, Abraham, Isaac and Jacob; then you have the law, and the land and the kingdom, the period of Christ's earthly ministry, and the post-Pentecost period. Whatever divisions are made, it is fairly standard stuff. But Darby's twist on it – the spin that he introduced – was to teach that *God dispensed his relationship to humanity on an entirely different basis during each of the seven dispensations.* Now, actually, you cannot read, for example, Romans 4 without discovering that, as far as St Paul was concerned, Abraham, who was a patriarch, was received into relationship with God on exactly the same basis as he, Paul, was. Therefore you and I, two thousand years later, have exactly the same relationship with God – on the basis of grace and the gift of righteousness – as did Abraham. And it is actually completely unscriptural to suggest that God dispenses his relationship to humanity in different ways. Darby also divided the future destiny of God's people. And you still find this taught in the books today, that actually the new heaven and the new earth are for two classes of people —that the Jews will be relegated to planet earth, whilst the Christians enjoy heaven. Now again, that just drives a coach and horses through Paul's teaching about the one Christ who has broken down all barriers between Jew and Gentile, and his teaching in Ephesians 2 that there is the one new creation —Jew and Gentile believing in the one Messiah, brought together, sharing eternity together. Scripture does not invite us to look down on Jews as people who have a lesser place in God's eternity. All people of God, trusting in Christ, will have the same destiny. When you read the New Testament, I find it difficult to understand why anybody believes a word that Darby wrote in this area —but there we are. His theories have become popular.

Why has the secret rapture been accepted by so many? Partly on the 'biblical' case that is made for it and partly because it is so immensely comforting. Moreover, there is that very proper, biblical challenge to be constantly ready, which provides a wholly appropriate impetus for holiness. If Jesus can return at any moment, then there is incredible pressure on non-believers to join in before it is too late. There is a sense in which there is a very proper urgency to preaching of the gospel, and the call to faith. It is certainly unbiblical to suggest that we are inviting hearers to a leisurely and infinitely prolonged consideration of God's call to them! I do however want to point out that the pressure generated by fear and anxiety is not a mark of New Testament evangelism, even though there is the clear element of being rescued or saved from something, e.g. in, "Save yourselves from this corrupt generation" (Acts 2:40). Nonetheless, the emphasis is not one of anxious panic! For Christians it is argued that there is enormous incentive to faith and holiness, if Christ can come again at any time. Again, that may well be good, in its own way, but the New Testament shows that our faith should be the result not of fear of the timing of Christ's return, but of awareness of the accountability for the way we have lived when he returns. So we are bound to ask the question: even if the teaching has achieved positive results in some areas, is it the truth? Is there a biblical case for the secret rapture? The answer is 'no'! I was quite surprised to learn this —knowing how securely established the teaching is in parts of the church. There is not one single clear statement in the New Testament to suggest that Christ will come secretly *for* the saints, and then visibly *with* the saints. 1 Thessalonians 4 and 5 speaks of the rapture, certainly, but gives no implication that it will be secret. So those who teach this position depend upon certain inferences which they detect in Scripture. Now, it seems to me that there is an immediate warning bell that goes off when I hear that sort of thing said. For when doctrine is built on inference, rather than on clear statement of Scripture, it seems there is a far greater danger of reading into Scripture what we want to see, rather than actually taking from Scripture what the Spirit placed there in the first place.

Consider these inferences. The first concerns imminence. It is suggested that statements within the New Testament about the imminence of Christ's appearing support the case. There is the repetition of the phrase 'coming soon' in the

Book of Revelation. In James 5:9, 'the Judge is standing at the door!'; Matthew 24:33 has the same image. Well, surely if somebody is standing at the door, the next stage in the drama is to step through it. Therefore Christ's coming must be near. But what does the Bible actually say? What does it actually mean by the words 'soon' and 'quickly'? Clearly, the sense must be relative, given that we have waited two thousand years. So to what (or to whom) does the timescale of 'soon' relate? We recall that the language of the New Testament relates to the nature and self-revelation of God. So in Psalm 90:4 we read that 'a thousand years' are 'like a day' to the Lord. The problem of interpreting the word 'soon' was there for the New Testament writers, as it is for us. So Peter writes,

> But do not forget this one thing, dear friends: With the Lord a day is like a thousand years, and a thousand years are like a day. The Lord is not slow in keeping his promise, as some understand slowness. He is patient with you, not wanting anyone to perish, but everyone to come to repentance.
>
> But the day of the Lord will come like a thief. The heavens will disappear with a roar; the elements will be destroyed by fire, and the earth and everything in it will be laid bare.
>
> Since everything will be destroyed in this way, what kind of people ought you to be? You ought to live holy and godly lives as you look forward to the day of God and speed its coming.
>
> *2 Peter 3:8–12a*

Again, the focus is on immediacy and readiness. We must learn to see time through God's eyes, as it were. We see how Peter teaches that the supposed 'slowness' is actually indicative of the mercy of God, whose will is that all should repent. The 'delay' is a cause for thankfulness for an opportunity given, rather than a concern that flows from our limited temporal perspective. The New Testament consistently acknowledges the reality of the 'delay'. We need only consider the parable concerning the return of the king which will take 'a long time'. (See Matthew 24–25). The imagery of 'harvest' in the teaching of Jesus also illustrates this. As any farmer knows, harvests take time to come about. A text which is often used by some who hold the secret rapture position is this, from James 5, 'Be patient and stand firm, because the Lord's coming is near'. But, clearly, the purpose of the verse is to inculcate patience rather than to set out a specific human timescale.

If the first 'inference' is imminence, the second is that the New Testament allegedly teaches that 'surprise' will characterise the event. We are reminded of the imagery of a 'thief', in 2 Peter 3, and in Matthew, when Jesus teaches both that no one knows the date, and that we are to keep watch. So, the argument runs, he can come at any moment. The Bible is certainly clear that time and date are unknown. However, that need not mean there will be no warning at all. The New Testament distinguishes on this point between believers and unbelievers. Consider the words of Paul in 1 Thessalonians 5:2–3, with which we began this chapter: '...you know very well that the day of the Lord will come like a thief in the night. While people are saying "Peace and safety", destruction will come on them suddenly, as labour pains on a pregnant woman, and they will not escape.' So there will be people for whom it is totally unexpected. But in the very next verse (v. 4) it is made clear that believers need not be surprised or shocked, 'But you, brothers, are not in darkness so that this day should surprise you like a thief.' Is that unfair? The fact is that Christian disciples, who are called to be faithful witnesses, need to know the truth. We are to make that truth known to our neighbours. The New Testament motivates us and informs us, so that we will be equipped to do so. So there is no unfairness here. Jesus frequently used the expression 'watch' in relation to End time events. Disciples are to look for the signs; they need to read the lesson of the fig tree. Why would he tell us to watch, if his coming will not be signalled by events which we might observe? The final sign Jesus mentions is highly visual: 'The sun will be dark, and the moon will not give its light. The stars will fall from the sky, and then the Son of Man will be seen coming on the clouds.' When Jesus used the phrase 'As it was in the days of Noah', we recall that in the days of Noah people were taken completely by surprise, but they nonetheless were given a sign, namely the construction of the ark! Noah and his wife were certainly not taken by surprise. Those who know and attend to the words of Scripture really should not be surprised when the moment comes.

The same principle can be applied here. So the New Testament does not support the concept of an 'any moment' rapture. But that in no way diminishes the call to believers to stay alert and watchful. There are countless scriptural encouragements to maintain this attitude. We want to be wise bridesmaids, not foolish ones.

A further alleged 'inference' proposed in support of the secret rapture theory is the notion that the language used in the New Testament implies that there is more than one event. The Greek uses three distinct terms: 'parousia', 'epiphaneia' and 'apocalypse'. The first of these expressions, parousia, was used of a king arriving in state outside his city. His courtiers would go out to greet him, and then they entered together. This summarises the New Testament teaching perfectly: believers, living and dead, will meet the Lord together. 'Epiphaneia' bore a connotation of salvation. A similar expression is employed in the Old Testament to signify the shekinah glory of God descending upon the tabernacle. There is a sense that God appears to save his people, just in time. 'Apocalypse', as we have seen, simply means unveiling. There will be a moment when Jesus will be seen as he is, in splendour and glory. In fact the three terms are deployed interchangeably. So, again, there is no justification for thinking that we are talking about different events.

We are also told by proponents of the secret rapture theory that the fact that the word 'church' (Gk. *ekklesia*) is not used in certain passages implies that Christians are secretly raptured before the tribulation. This is one of the weakest arguments. It implies that the words 'elect' and 'saints' refer only to believing Jews still on earth at the coming of Christ. But all the relevant passages are directly addressed to Christians. In Matthew 24, for instance, the words 'elect' and 'saints' are the normal collective nouns signifying Christians. Moreover, if they really only apply to Jews in Revelation 4 to 18, then how is it that they suddenly refer to Christians again in Revelation 22? Six of the epistles in the New Testament are written without the word 'church' appearing in them.

Neither John 14, nor 1 Corinthians 15, nor the passage quoted at the beginning of this chapter contain the word church. Nor is the word used in the description of the new Jerusalem in Revelation 21. We could also ask why, if Christians are not on earth during the tribulation, Jesus teaches his disciples so vividly about it? And why would Revelation call for patient endurance from the saints?

A further supposed 'inference' centres on the issue of 'wrath'. Christians, we are told, are exempt from the wrath of God which is connected with the great tribulation. We recall Romans 5:9; 1 Thessalonians 5:9 ('For God did not appoint us to suffer wrath but to receive salvation through our Lord Jesus Christ'); and Revelation 3:10, which promises "I will also keep you from the hour of trial that is going to come upon the whole world to test those who live on the earth." Yet Christians are not immune from the everyday tragedies of life. We suffer along with anybody else. Jesus quite clearly predicted tribulation for his followers in John 16:33, "In this world you will have trouble". In 2 Timothy 3:12, Paul says, 'In fact, everyone who wants to live a godly life in Christ Jesus will be persecuted.' The word 'tribulation' occurs fifty times in the New Testament, and only three apply to this final period of tribulation. Further, if we take Romans chapter 1 seriously, we know that we already live in a world that is experiencing the wrath of God. Look at what happened to the church at Philadelphia in Revelation 3. The promise to keep the church from the hour of trial cannot actually be linked to the end of the world, because that church in Philadelphia no longer exists!

Finally, we are assured by its proponents that the secret rapture theory gives comfort, as well as promoting faithfulness. As we remarked earlier, there is a comfortable feeling about being removed from harm's way, but can a false doctrine provide worthwhile comfort? Jesus taught that the truth sets us free. However comforting something which is not the truth may appear, it can lead to bondage and captivity.

The only worthwhile hope is founded on revealed truth. True comfort is only to be found in Christ's promise to be with us when the trial comes: "In this world, you will have trouble. But take heart! I have overcome the world" (John 16:33).

It is the whole truth we need, not just part of it. "In this world, you will have trouble" —well, that is truth. But, "I have overcome..." —that is the whole truth. One might ask what would be the point of anything in the Book of Revelation from chapter 6 onwards if the last generation of Christians at the time of the second coming were to be removed before the great tribulation.

If the truth is given to set us free, the implication is that falsehood, or even a distortion of the truth, will in some way restrict or damage our ability to follow our Lord faithfully. I am convinced that the popular teaching on the subject of the rapture in the church of today is unbiblical, and therefore dangerous. I believe it to be the single most likely cause of the huge falling away from the faith which Jesus predicted among his followers at the End —see Matthew 24:9–14. Here Jesus explicitly predicts persecution of the Christian community throughout the world with the consequence that 'many will turn away'. Clearly, there has been persecution of the church throughout the ages since it was born on the day of Pentecost, and persecution remains a fact of life for countless of my Christian brothers and sisters throughout the world as I write. If, as I believe, this persecution will reach an unprecedented level in the last days and years of earth history, then true, biblical teaching as to what we are to expect is vital. I believe that the Book of Revelation – in accord with Jesus' own clear teaching in the last week of his earthly ministry – prepares the Christians of earth's final generation for unimaginable trials. It calls for patient endurance; it encourages Christians to stand firm. If Christians have swallowed false teaching, and believe that God will pluck them from harm's way just in time, how will they stand when tribulation comes? I fear that many who have been falsely taught will abandon their faith —the terrible irony is that they will do so believing God to have broken a promise he has not in fact made. He does promise to be with us always, even amid the storm. Nowhere in Scripture does he promise to remove us from the storm.

Lord, keep me firm in the hope you have set before me. Thank you for your promise to be with me always, even to the end of the world. Guard me from turning away from you. Keep me faithful in whatever times of trial I may face, knowing that you have overcome the world. Reign in me always, O sovereign of my heart. Amen.

12

THE MILLENNIUM

The issue of the millennium has been a focus of much controversy amongst Christians. It is certainly one of the most controversial of all the issues surrounding the End times. When Jesus returns, will there be either a literal thousand years – or, at any rate, a lengthy period – when this earth is governed by Christ and the saints? That is the much debated question. The biblical millennium, mentioned six times in Revelation 20, has dogged the church as an issue for centuries. I want to look at it within a framework of five major questions about the return of Christ: Who? Where? How? When? and Why? We are going to be looking, essentially, at the two chapters 19 and 20.

'I saw heaven standing open...' (Revelation 19:11). What a glorious privilege John is granted. In reading Revelation, we have become accustomed now to looking for sevens. Now we notice that the whole book ends with another series of visions —a sevenfold series. Notice in the first half of chapter 19, verses 1 to 10, that John *hears*. To go through the Book of Revelation marking each time John says 'I heard' or 'I saw' can really help you to see more clearly the pattern that unfolds. And in verses 1 and 6, John hears things in heaven. But from verse 11 onwards, in 19:11 to 21:1, there is a sevenfold series of visions. Here they are:

1. The rider on the white horse, riding out of heaven's open door.

2. The angel that invites the birds of the earth to a rather macabre supper of human flesh, the battle of Armageddon (first mentioned in chapter 16).

3. Then the angel binding Satan 'for a thousand years'.

4. Then the mention of the first resurrection —dead Christians being raised to reign on earth with Christ for a thousand years, after which Satan is released for a final fling, before being destroyed.

5. Then the great white throne appears (20:11).

6. Then the second resurrection brings all people to life for the final judgment, before which earth disappears —it flees away.

7. Then the new heaven and the new earth appear.

Those are the seven things that John sees, with which the Book of Revelation closes. So let us begin our questions.

Who? Who is going to return? You may think that is a strange thing to ask. But actually people have all sorts of odd ideas about who is coming back. I want to start with that verse Acts 1:11, which has the angels talking to the disciples, who are standing, rather forlornly on the day of the ascension. The angel asks them why they are looking up into the sky. "This same Jesus, who has been taken from you into heaven, will come back in the same way you have seen him go into heaven." It is very significant that the angels choose – of all the names that have been ascribed to Christ – this human name, Jesus. It is a great encouragement to me to know that, when Jesus returns, he will not have changed. It is one of our fears as humans that when we say farewell to somebody we are not going to see for a long time, we worry that they will be different when we see them again. What will have changed between us? Will they be different? Will I be different? Well, when Jesus returns, he will not be different. He will still be fully man and fully God.

In passing, we note that the church has struggled, over the centuries, to hold together Christ's humanity and his divinity. There is still the feeling around that, when Christ came to earth, he took human form for thirty odd years, and then discarded it like an old suit, as soon as he returned to heaven. But that is not what the New Testament teaches. It teaches that, in heaven, seated on the throne, is one who bears the scars of human rejection. The incarnation – which is the technical phrase used when we talk about God becoming man – was permanent. God, who set galaxies spinning in the universe, came to earth, entered this world in the most fragile way —as a little baby. We so easily miss the impact of that when we think about these things at Christmas. And the human life of Jesus is recorded for us in our Gospels. We read of a unique human being whose eyes filled with tears of compassion for the oppressed, and yet blazed with anger against the oppressor; whose hands could lift the weak and the fallen, and yet could whip the greedy; a man who was loved by sinners, yet hated by hypocrites; adored by the poor, yet feared by the powerful. It is this Jesus who comes again. The thing that will be different from most of his life on earth is that he will have his glorified, exalted resurrection body when he comes.

Paul talks about this resurrection body – 'his glorious body' – and we will have transformed bodies like it. (See Philippians 3:21), but his glorious body bears the scars of crucifixion.

According to the writer to the Hebrews (2:9), Jesus is our pioneer in experiencing resurrection. In 1 Corinthians 15, Paul gives us the clearest teaching in the New Testament about the new resurrection body. Yes, it is very significant that the angels identify that it is Jesus who is returning. 'Who is coming back?' is a fairly uncontroversial question.

Where? It seems reasonable to think that if Jesus is to return bodily, then it must be to a specific location. The Bible shows quite clearly that Jesus is going to return to a very specific place —a mountain refuge that, even today, the nations of the world will not recognise, refusing to open embassies there. Since 1000BC, this particular city has been besieged 46 times, partially destroyed 32 times, and burnt to the ground 5 times —amazingly, it is called the city of peace. Jesus called it the city of the Great King. (See Matthew 5). In the Book of Revelation, John refers to it as the great city. The Old Testament prophets foresaw a day when the nations of the world would look to Jerusalem for the settlement of international disputes, for leadership into peace. Christ will return to Jerusalem, the city he loves. In Isaiah 2 and Micah 4, we see these great promises of swords being beaten into pruning hooks —the peace of God spreading through the world. Jerusalem is strategically ideal. It sits, quite literally, and quite specifically, at the very centre of the world's land mass. It sits at the meeting point of the three great continents of Europe, Africa and Asia. The Bible is even more precise than that about the location of Christ's return. Having been seen by every human living on the planet, Christ will actually – I believe – place his resurrection feet on the Mount of Olives. He ascended from the Mount of Olives where, just a few weeks earlier, the crowds had lauded him with palm branches, as he rode into the city on a donkey. The prophet Zechariah, in chapter 9 of his prophecy, foresaw Christ the king entering Jerusalem on a donkey; and later, in chapter 14, he says of that day (which we know, by now, is shorthand for all the biblical writers for the final day of earth history) —'on that day, his feet will stand on the Mount of Olives.'

How? How is it all going to happen? There will be a huge contrast between the first and second comings. Think once again of the nativity. For nine months, Jesus was hidden inside Mary's womb. Aside from the relatives who were waiting for Mary to give birth, Christ's coming was unknown, except to the eye of faith that looked for the Messiah. As far as nearly everyone was concerned, Mary's pregnancy was no more significant than any other pregnancy on the face of the planet at the time. In human terms, the king of the Jews was only born in David's royal city because some distant emperor had a newfangled idea called the poll tax. Jesus' cradle was an animal's feeding trough. His birth went completely unnoticed, except by a few shepherds, until some sages from the East (probably descendants of the Jews who had stayed in Babylon after the exile, who knew from the sacred Scriptures what to look for) arrived, following a single star, whose meaning was only significant to those who could read it. It was as though God wanted to slip into the world with minimal publicity —no fanfare; a brief display in the heavens, seen by a few shepherds. What a contrast with the second coming: visible, audible, tangible. He will come not as a helpless baby, but the Lord of every creature; not with just a single star in the sky, but with lightning flashing from east to west; not alone, but with tens of thousands of angels and with all the saints of God; not quietly this time, with the sounds of a newborn, but with the trumpet of God. 'Look,' says John in Revelation 1:7, 'he is coming with the clouds, and every eye will see him, even those who pierced him; and all the peoples of the earth will mourn because of him. So shall it be! Amen.' Look, too, at 1 Thessalonians 4:16, the 'noisiest' verse in the Bible, talking of Christ's return. There will be no mistake, when Christ comes again. Nobody will need to ask the questions: 'Where?' and 'Who?'

Of course, the question we return to is 'When?' Daniel depicts the asking of this question: "How long will it be before these astonishing things are fulfilled?" (Daniel 12:6). How often we want to ask the same question! It is ironic that there have been so many disputes and so much controversy over this question, when we have actually discovered in our studies that John, and the Spirit who revealed Revelation to him, actually had the least interest in 'when'. I have set this question of the millennium here, toward the close of our study, in the hope that we can be more excited by the certainty of who is coming, rather than getting bogged down in the matter of when. But we have been told a few things. First of all, no-one knows precisely when he will return. We have been told that there will be signs, and we looked at that in an earlier chapter. Many of these signs will recur. Daniel himself said that war will continue until the End. Revelation does suggest increasing intensity in the signs as history moves on. Revelation 15:1 – just to give one example – talks about the seven plagues, the last plagues: 'for with them, God's wrath is completed.' So there is a sense of increasing intensity in the build-up toward the end of earth history. Many believe that earth history will end in a particularly awful, but short, period, known as the great tribulation, or the great trouble. Jesus talks about it in Matthew 24. It will be a very limited period. Jesus taught that if these days had not been kept short – which they have been for the sake of the elect – none would stand. Many believe that they will last 3½ years. This is not, I suggest, an absolute cornerstone of faith, but we need to be aware of that position. In Daniel 7 we are shown an image, a vision of the beasts —interestingly, again, coming up out of the sea, as was the beast in Revelation, we saw earlier. In verse 21, the particular beast is waging war against the saints and defeating them, and again, at the end of verse 22, '...the time came when they possessed the kingdom.' Verse 25 continues about the beast, probably the End time beast: 'He will speak against the Most High and oppress his saints and try to change the set times and the laws. The saints will be handed over to him for a time, times and half a time' – that's biblical speak for 3½ years.

Part of the problems with these references in Daniel is that they are explicitly linked to the destruction of the temple, because they are linked to the time when the daily sacrifice would end. But it is interesting that in Matthew 24, when Jesus is talking about the destruction of the temple, he uses that very event as a sign of the End. So based on that, and also on these verses in Revelation (which also refer to a period of 3½ years – 1260 days – remember the ancients worked in years of 360), there is a strong sense within the church that, at the very end of time, when Satan is at his most desperate, all hell will break loose —as you would expect. And there are various references in Revelation to a very severe period of tribulation for the church, 3½ years before the actual end comes. I suggest that we do not spend our time worrying about what the details of that tribulation may be, but that, actually, we spend our time – if we are going to study the Scriptures – fortifying ourselves in the knowledge that God will be with us and will stand by us, whatever comes.

So what do we make of the millennium? How do we read Revelation 20? Essentially, there are three positions. There are so many variations within them; but essentially they are amillennialism, pre-millennialism, and post-millennialism. In post-millennialism, it is said that Jesus will return after the millennium – which may be a literal thousand years – during which time Christians will literally rule the earth. This idea is behind some of the ideas of forming Christian parties, and so on —the idea that Christians will take over the globe – or at least the majority of governments – and that then Christ will return. It is a largely discredited position today. I would find it very difficult, I think, to foresee that. Certainly in Matthew 24, Jesus gives no hint whatsoever of this sort of worldwide dominance. The two main positions are amillennialism and pre-millennialism.

Amillennialism goes right back to Augustine. Basically, this position is that there is no thousand year rule of Christ on the earth when he returns, but that we are now living in the millennium. Proponents of this view point to the fact that, in Revelation 20, John sees thrones, which up until that point have always been in heaven; he sees souls reigning —and souls are always in heaven. The major problem for the amillennial position lies in the opening verses of Revelation 20. Satan is banished. Now five very strong verbs are used to describe what this angel does to Satan: he seizes, chains, throws, locks, seals —the picture we get is of Satan completely removed from the sphere of earth history. Can we really argue that we are living in that period today? Was Satan really bound at Auschwitz or in apartheid? I would find that position very difficult to hold with conviction.

Pre-millennialism is the oldest of the views. It holds that Jesus will return and will reign for a lengthy period – maybe for a literal thousand years – on this earth, before the final judgment and before the revelation of the new heaven and the new earth. It is not an issue over which to go to the stake, or to fall out with other believers. But if I were forced to plump for one position, it would be this one. I suspect that when Jesus returns and we see him for ourselves, this is just not going to be an issue; but we need to know, as clearly as possible, what the Bible teaches.

Why do I find this view the most convincing of the three principal ones? There are several reasons. It is the oldest view, and I always tend to give particular weight to positions that can be traced all the way back to the Church Fathers, better still to the apostles. This view was unchallenged until the time of Augustine. But more significantly, perhaps, and in contrast with Augustine's world-denying tendencies, the pre-millennial position does justice to the biblical doctrine of God as Creator of a universe with which he was pleased, and with which he has not yet finished, and which he wants to transform. Judaism and Christianity are very earthy religions in the healthiest possible sense. It is also the case that this view fits the plain pattern of Revelation 20, and the plain sense of the text itself: the second coming, the millennial reign on earth, the judgment day and the new creation. A thousand years is specified six times – John is emphasising that. The focus throughout is on earth – Jesus rides out of heaven and comes to earth for the battle of Armageddon and the thrones appear, and so on – everything is focused on earth. The beast and the false prophet have been destroyed at the end of Revelation 19, and we know that the beast and the false prophet represent the corrupt government of our planet, so there is a political vacuum. So who steps in? Christ and the saints. The thrones appear (20:4) with the saints ruling, with the purpose of administering justice. But what a vindication and compensation for those who have been beheaded by a corrupt world order —to sit on thrones administering true justice for the planet. And most clearly of all (20:4), the souls of the departed come to life. You will see that that phrase occurs twice, once in verse 4 and once in verse 5. The great flaw with the amillennial position is its claim that verse 4 refers to *spiritual* regeneration at the point of death as believers enter the heavenly kingdom, but in verse 5 this phrase refers to *physical* resurrection. In actual fact it is always used of physical resurrection, and to say that it means one thing in one verse and one thing in the next verse, without any other reason, is to break the first law of reading the Bible: you take it in its plain sense, unless you are clearly told not to do so. It is the verb used of Lazarus in John 11, when Lazarus is raised from the dead. This view is supported elsewhere in the Scriptures. Just to pick out a few references: three times in Revelation, John talks of the 'overcomers', the saints ruling the nations; Paul writes to the Corinthians: 'Do you not know that you will rule the world, that you will judge the world?' Surely this is referring to these thrones in Revelation 20. We sing the song based on Philippians 2:10f., that one day every knee will bow, every tongue will confess.... When is that to be, if not on earth? This idea of a first resurrection and a second resurrection is there elsewhere in Scripture. And that is what Revelation teaches here. Paul writes to Timothy, '...if we endure, we will also reign with him' (2 Timothy 2:12). That is a perfect summary of the whole Book of Revelation. If we endure, we will reign with him. In Acts 1:6, the disciples, just before his ascension, ask Jesus, "Lord, are you at this time going to restore the kingdom to Israel?" They understood the kingdom to be an earthly, political rule in God's perfect time, according to David's dynasty. Jesus did not say, 'Don't be silly.' He just told them that it was not for them to know times or dates. When can a descendant of David sit on David's throne and rule forever, if not in the millennium? If it is not then, the New Testament gives us no other answer. In the Gospels, Gabriel tells Mary that her son will be given the throne of his father David. Jesus is born king of the Jews and dies with that title displayed on the cross. Think of Jesus' teaching on prayer: "...Your kingdom come, your will be done on earth as it is in heaven...." When did Jesus think that was going to be? And the Old Testament is full of prophecies about a time when God himself would rule the earth in peace and righteousness and harmony and justice. (See Isaiah 2,

Micah 4, Zechariah 14.) The Lord will be king over the whole earth. (See Psalm 72); and, '...the earth will be full of the knowledge of the LORD, as the waters cover the sea.' (See Isaiah 11:9.) All this becomes clearer when we ask our final question, 'Why?'

Why is Jesus coming back? It is by far the most important question to answer, yet it is the most neglected. Why does Jesus need to come back? Why does the earth need his return? What can he only do by returning? What will he yet do here, that he was not able to do the first time he was here? What can he only do on earth that he cannot do from his position in heaven?

Firstly, to 'complete' the work of salvation. Many Christians think of salvation as an instantaneous thing. Yet the New Testament frequently talks of it as a process. The New Testament uses the verb 'save' in three tenses: we have been saved; we are being saved, and we will be saved. The second of those tenses is continuous, ongoing. Theologians use the terms justification, sanctification and glorification. The process only reaches its goal when salvation in the third, final sense is completed. People who mistakenly think that nothing physical can be truly good may think of floating around as a disembodied soul, but that will not do for those who really capture the truth and vision revealed in the New Testament. Hebrews 9:28 says that Jesus will return again '...not to bear sin, but to bring salvation for those who are waiting for him.' And as far as the New Testament is concerned, salvation in the last sense of the word will not be fully completed until our bodies are transformed. (See 1 John 3:2.) Salvation is not complete now for any Christian —even including those who have died. When Paul looks at the state of the dead before Christ's return, he talks of them being unclothed, imperfect, unfinished. Paul witnesses to the struggles we know of trying to live the new life of the Spirit in the old body. 'What a wretched man I am!' And, 'I delight in God's law; but I see another law at work in the members of my body...' (Romans 7). Then he says in Romans 8:23, '... we, ourselves, who have the first fruits of the Spirit, groan inwardly as we wait eagerly for our adoption as sons, the redemption of our bodies.' How ironic it is that, because we have the Spirit, we long for new bodies. The final act of salvation, the final act of restoration, the final climax of Christian hope, is the gift to you of a new body, a body that is unstained by sin, unlimited in its expression of the life of the Spirit, and completely unfettered by the processes of age, decay and disease. Our body will be like his glorious body. That is good news. I say often that if you want to see for whom our world has good news, look in the magazines —you see it is the young, the trendy, the beautiful, the rich. The world has no good news for the chronically ill, for those who, at this moment, are dying, for those who are suffering the fragility of the human body. The Christian faith does. The Christian faith offers good news for everybody, no matter how crippled, how fragile, how near death: the good news of a new body to come.

Secondly, Christ will come back to be vindicated. Again, it makes sense that, if every knee is to bow, then Christ is to come back to the arena where knees refused to bow. If Christ is to be seen as the risen Lord of glory, he needs to come back to the very place where he was ejected from this world by human rebellion and crucifixion. That is one of the reasons he is coming back to Jerusalem —that is where he was rejected; that is where he will reign, whether we like it or not. Finally, he will come back to conquer evil and to judge the wicked. Possibly we get in these last two the reason – strange as it may seem – for Satan's temporary release. For me, this is one serious difficulty with the pre-millennial position: the idea that Satan is released at the end of the millennium. (20:7.) Many people today find it hard to see Christ as judge, even though he told us that all judgment has been committed to him. But if Christ comes back and rules this earth for a lengthy period of time with the saints, in peace and harmony and justice, where evil is banished, and if at the end of that time the nations of the world still rejoin Satan in rebelling against that rule, then it will have been shown once again that judgment is absolutely warranted. When the great white throne then appears, everyone will have to acknowledge that the judgment is just.

No matter which view of the millennium verses you personally find convincing, the thing you need to hold on to here is the wonder of that complete salvation which accompanies Christ's return. Go on praying, 'Your kingdom come, your will be done, on earth as in heaven.'

I want to leave you with some very comforting words that one of Daniel's angels left him with, words which close his book: "As for you, go your way till the end. You will rest, and then at the end of the days you will rise to receive your allotted inheritance."

Heavenly Father, we praise you that, in Christ, you brought salvation to a fallen world. We praise you that, through faith in his blood, you have begun in us that process of transformation which will one day lead to us receiving our new bodies.

Lord, we ask you for faith and grace to long for your coming, to long for the day when you will bring to fulfilment the finished work of salvation in us, when we will no longer struggle with the temptations and the sins of this life, when we will no longer struggle against the disease and the decay and the death that we see all around us. Lord, we want to soar in our new bodies with you.

O Father, we do pray that your Son will come again soon. Come, Lord Jesus. Amen.

Appendix 1

END TIMES CHART

God the Creator

The Heavens (Angels)

The Intermediate State (Hades/Sheol)

The Earth

New Heaven

New Earth

Hell

The Intermediate State (Hades/Sheol)

The Life
Death
Resurrection
and
Ascension
of
Christ
Pentecost

The Present Age
(the Age of the Spirit)
Signs of the Times
(Wars, rumours of war)
(natural disaster)
(persecution of the church)
(proclamation of the gospel)
(beasts, false prophets, antichrists)

The Last Days
(Intensification)
(The Beast)
(Antichrist)
(Tribulation)
(cosmic distress)

The Return
(Mt 24; Rev 19)
(Dead in Christ rise)
(Rapture)
(New bodies)
(*Millennium*)
(*2nd Resurrection*)
(Judgment)
(Destruction of present cosmos)

Appendix 2

NEW TESTAMENT REFERENCES TO THE END
(outside the Book of Revelation)

Matthew 12:28f; 21:33–46; 22:1–14; 24:1–25:46.
Mark 13:1–37; 14:62.
Luke 10:18; 21:5–36; 14:16–24.
John 5:27; 14:1–3.
Acts 1:7; 1:11; 2:17 (quoting Joel 2:28); 3:20; 7:56; 17:31.
Romans 2:28f; 8:18–39; 9:6–8; 9:3–33; 10:1–4; 10:9–13; 11.
1 Corinthians 9:27; 15:35–50; 15:51–57; 15:58.
2 Corinthians 5:1–10.
Galatians 3:28; 6:15.
Ephesians 2:11–22.
Philippians 1:21–23; 3:20f.
Colossians 3:1–17; 3:11.
1 Thessalonians 4:13–5:11.
2 Thessalonians 2.
1 Timothy 4:1–4.
2 Timothy 2:11–13; 3:1–9; 3:12–14; 4:1–8.
Titus 2:13.
Hebrews 1:10–12 (quoting Psalm 102:25–27); 2:2; 2:3; 6:4–8; 9:27; 9:28; 11:9–10; 11:13–16; 12:1; 12:22–29; 13:14.
James 5:8f.
1 Peter 1:3–7; 2:9–12. (Hosea 2:23; Romans 9:25f); 3:19f; 4:7; 4:12; 5:4.
2 Peter 3:3–18. (See Psalm 90:4.)
1 John 2:18–27.
2 John 7 & 8.
Jude 6 (cf. Revelation 20:1ff); 14f; 18f; 20f.